Origin
of the
Templars

And Origin of the
Vatican's Power

Origin
of the
Templars

And Origin of the
Vatican's Power

Sanford Holst

SANTORINI
BOOKS

Santorini Publishing
14622 Ventura Boulevard, #800
Los Angeles, California 91403

First Edition
1st Printing: September 2017

Publisher's Cataloging-In-Publication Data

Holst, Sanford.
   Origin of the Templars: and origin of the
Vatican's power / Sanford Holst.

   p. : ill. ; cm.
   Includes bibliographical references and index.
   ISBN: 978-1-945199-00-4

   1. Templars—History. 2. Military religious
orders—History. 3. Crusades. I. Title.

HS403 .H65 2017
366/.1   2017912956

Contents

"The Templars are most excellent soldiers. They wear white mantles with a red cross, and when they go to the wars a standard of two colours called (Beauceant) is borne before them. They go in silence. Their first attack is the most terrible. In going they are the first, in returning the last[1]."

Malcolm Barber
quoting an anonymous pilgrim

Fig. 1 Knight Templar in Spain

Chapter 1

Arise, Sir Knight

$\mathcal{P}$ennants flew and crowds cheered on the boisterous day in August of 1096 when Godfrey of Bouillon led a sea of knights and infantry out of the borderlands between France and Germany to begin the First Crusade. Among the many dedicated young knights believed to be in Godfrey's service during those early days was Hugh de Payens, who would go on to form the Knights Templar and serve as their first Grand Master.[2]

Godfrey joined three other armies from different parts of Europe and together they marched to the Holy Land to free Jerusalem from the Muslims who held it. As Addison,[3] Barber[4] and others have told us, many adventures and battles lay along Godfrey's path before he became the first Christian king of Jerusalem.[5]

Yet beyond all the events enumerated in traditional treatments of the Templars, the Crusades, and the rising power of the Vatican, many intriguing mysteries remain.

Why were the Knights Templar so secretive, and how was that attribute used to help them achieve their legendary successes?

These knights were not businessmen, and had even taken vows of poverty—so what were the unforeseen opportunities that enabled them to become the sophisticated bankers of Europe?

Saint Bernard left the comfort of his abbey in France to help nine common knights in Jerusalem establish a new religious order *different than his own.* Why would he do such a thing?

The Count of Champagne stood second in power only to the king of France, and chose to give his support to the first Templars at critical times during their inception. What drove him to take such a deep interest in these knights?

Clearly the growing power of the pope contributed to the rise of the Templars to their enviable position of influence in Europe and the Middle East. But the Vatican was only swampy ground with a church and graveyard on it for a large part of its existence. How did this patch of ground turn into a worldwide center of power adorned with priceless artworks and other evidence of great wealth?

The pope was virtually without power for many centuries—and was not even the most influential Christian bishop—yet on the eve of the Crusades he was powerful enough to summon kings and knights to fight for his chosen cause. The emperor of the Byzantine Empire who had requested this help from the pope was the main sponsor of the Eastern Orthodox Church, the pope's most bitter rival. What motivated the pope to act against his own declared interests in that way?

It is important to recognize the severe problems faced by the Crusaders, the pope and the first Templars in order to appreciate how difficult it was for them to accomplish the high level of wealth and power they achieved.

When the First Crusade was announced, most of the people in Europe were struggling to keep a roof over their head or to fend off militant neighbors. Yet they responded in overwhelming numbers to risk death fighting strangers in a strange land. Why would they do that? We are told they wanted to help the few pilgrims going to the Holy Land, and gain spiritual benefits. That cannot possibly explain the incredible outpouring of volunteers which happened. As it turns out, there was another key motivator at play, without which the Crusades might not have taken place at all. The stories behind all these grand events are some of the most intriguing that we encounter.

One of the great climactic moments that led to the creation of the Knights Templar—and even the creation of knighthood, the Crusades and the power of the Vatican—happened in 711 AD. This was when a Muslim invasion was launched that swept across all of Spain and into the edge of France.[6] That foreign conquest put the prospect of having to fight against Islamic people right on the doorstep of the nations of Europe. And it did so in a way they could not possibly ignore.

This earth-shaking event would change the way European warfare was conducted, reshape countries, and contribute critically necessary elements to the creation of the Knights Templar and the steady rise in the power of the pope.

Chapter 2

The Muslim Conquest
Of Spain

When the Muslim general Tariq ibn Ziyad captured Tangier in Morocco during the year 710 AD, it completed the Islamic conquest of North Africa. But he had no time to rest, because just to the north of him across the Strait of Gibraltar the kingdom of Hispania—today known as the lands of Spain and Portugal—fell into civil war that same year. It was too great a prize to resist. A timely invitation from a Hispanic nobleman offering to help with that invasion pushed him into action, and the conquest of Spain began the following year.

Gibbon[7] described how Hispania, the Roman colony that covered all of the Iberian peninsula of Europe, fell to the Visigoths by 476 AD when the last emperor of the Western Roman Empire was overthrown. But over time the new masters had been converted to an early form of Christianity and their kingdom became quite civilized.[8]

When their king died in the year 710, however, one of his distant relatives known as Roderick usurped the crown and took the south and west of the country for himself. The legitimate heir, Achila II, kept the northern and eastern reaches. They did not know it at the time, but a critically important aspect of this split

Fig. 2   Map of Western Europe and North Africa at 732 AD

was that Roderick kept the small but powerful outpost of Ceuta on the shore of North Africa that the Muslims had been unable to capture.

Count Julian, the master of Ceuta, sent his daughter Florinda to King Roderick's capital city of Toledo, where she was to be educated or held as a hostage—or possibly both. Then an event took place upon which the fate of nations sometimes turn. Roderick raped Florinda.[9]

Julian immediately brought his daughter home. Then, in a furious rage, he contacted the Muslim general in Tangiers and offered to transport the man's troops across the Strait to Spain, and hide them at Julian's other fort near Gibraltar. All he asked in return was that vengeance be visited upon Roderick. Tariq accepted, and the invasion was on.

Ancient sources tell us that 1,700 soldiers were transported in Julian's boats, which shuttled back and forth across the Strait. When that whole force was assembled at Gibraltar, it set out against the local towns with great success. Roderick, upon hearing of these attacks, came south with a large number of infantry, and met the Moorish force at the Guadalete River. There he was apparently killed and his army dispersed.

It should be mentioned that the name *Moors* was applied to the invaders because they came from the country around Tangier that the Romans had called Mauritania. The people of that land were known as Mauri. Over time, Europeans simply called them Moors.[10]

When the Muslim governor of North Africa heard of Tariq's great victory in Spain, he rushed northward with reinforcements so that the campaign could continue. The cities of Seville and Cadiz fell quickly, and within a year the capital city of Toledo was also taken. Since Madrid did not yet exist at this time it was not on the casualty list, but it soon would be established about forty-five miles north of Toledo.

The path of conquest continued to the north and east until all of the Iberian peninsula had been taken except for a patch along the northern coast known as Asturias. It even included the capture of Barcelona and a piece of Southern France. All of these lands together were now called al-Andalus by the conquerors.

Fig. 3 Moorish soldiers campaigning in Spain

And their advances kept penetrating deeper into the land we know as France, until the Muslim forces were finally stopped by Charles Martel during 732 AD in an epic battle.

Charles Martel was the military leader of the Franks, a tribe that had settled in the north of what would become known as France, and gave their name to that country. They worked their way southward until they controlled almost all of the land in that modern nation. At the urging of his wife, their king converted to Christianity in 496 AD. Thereafter, the Franks and the people of Spain anchored what would become the Christian countries of Europe.

The weak king of the Franks, Theodoric IV, left all matters of state to Charles Martel. So it became his responsibility to some-how gather enough military forces to block the advancing Muslim armies.

Those Islamic troops had been led northward from al-Andalus by Abdul Rahman Al Ghafiqi. He quickly sacked Bordeaux then continued northward, winning many battles along the way. The secret to the Muslim successes seem to have been their well-trained cavalry, which literally rode over the various infantries sent against them.

Aware of that cavalry's success, Charles tried a different plan when it came time to fight the decisive Battle of Tours against them. He heavily armed his best soldiers, giving each of them up to 75 pounds of armor.[11] Then he kept them close together to sup-port each other. These knights-on-foot were able to turn back the Muslim cavalry. Then they slaughtered the lightly-armed Muslim infantry, killing the Islamic leader Abdul Rahman in the process.

It was a resounding victory against the invaders, and sent them fleeing back to Spanish land. The Muslim troops would never again reach that far into Europe.

And Charles had found a new military weapon: his knights. This weapon would be used extensively by his famous grandson, Charlemagne, who placed them on horseback. Those mounted knights would sweep all of Europe before them. But that was still several years in the future.

While Charles Martel was leading Christian forces to victory over the invading Moors, the pope in Rome was essentially powerless. He had some modest income as a bishop, because Christians would donate a piece of land from time to time which helped support their local church and priest. Any excess funds flowed upward to the bishop, and was used to support him and his work, including charity. Since the Bishop of Rome was also the pope, this source of revenue was called the *patrimony of Saint Peter*, and included some donations from outside his diocese. But these were held only as a local property owner. The pope had no ruling power over these lands.

In fact, the pope had almost no authority of any kind in Christian Europe, or even within the Church. The conversions of Northern people to Christianity had happened without his involvement. He was simply the bishop of Rome, and as the heir to Saint Peter he had some dignity and a theoretical role in religious matters. But the major power and influence within the Church was held by the bishops of Jerusalem and Antioch in the Holy Land, and by the bishop of Alexandria in Egypt. The Roman emperor in the East, situated in his capital city of Constantinople, used his power to support those Eastern leaders.

The most visible things which the pope had in his favor were the gifts given to his predecessor in the time of emperor Constantine. One of those was the marshlands known as the Vatican, which was the site of a cemetery. Since Saint Peter was buried there, Constantine ordered a large basilica church be built on that spot, with the altar placed directly over Peter's grave. The emperor also generously donated to the ongoing popes the ownership and use of the Lateran palace in the center of Rome. And beside that lavish home was built another large basilica church, this one for use by the pope in his role as the Bishop of Rome. These things gave the pope a nice residence, but a fairly meager existence.

As Bishop of Rome, he had a small curia—a group of administrators—to manage the affairs of the local diocese and the property that it owned, just like any other bishop. But that was all. There was no curia for the worldwide Church. The Vatican was just a church with a graveyard and a small residence for when the pope was there. It was far from being a center of power in any possible way.

Charlemagne Conquers, the Pope Rises

In many battles Charles Martel proved to be a great general and authority figure who greatly strengthened the kingdom of the Franks. But he did another thing as well. He became an admirer of Saint Boniface, and saw to it that his sons received a complete education at the hands of the only literate people at the time—Christian clergy. When Charles passed away in 741, his son Pepin kept in touch with the pope in Rome. And Pepin's son—the famous Charlemagne—did the same. This turned out to be a highly beneficial arrangement for the popes and kings involved.

That happened because the pope's diocese in Rome was basically surrounded by the Lombards, a northern tribe that swept into Italy in 568 AD. The invaders had converted to Christianity, so that was not an issue. But it meant that the Lombards ruled almost all of the Italian peninsula except for a strip of land that ran from Rome diagonally northward across the mountains to Ravenna on the shore of the Adriatic Sea. That strip of land was theoretically under the protection of the Byzantine emperor in Constantinople, but that did not stop the Lombards. In 751 AD they sacked Ravenna and then cast their eyes on Rome.

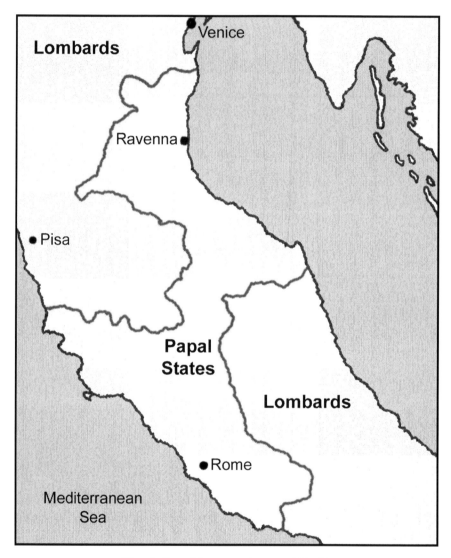

Fig. 4   Papal States in the year 800 AD

Pope Zachary desperately needed a savior, and turned northward to Pepin and the Franks.

Pepin was busy expanding the territory of the Franks, just as his father had done. But unlike his father he had no tolerance for the do-nothing kings who were nominally at the head of his people. Before eliminating Childeric III, the last king, Pepin decided to share any blame for this deed by consulting with Pope Zachary, even though the religious leader had no real authority in the matter. Given the threat at his doorstep from the Lombards, Zachary was happy to give his support to this proposal. So Pepin pushed Childeric into a monastery and took the title of king for himself. The revered Saint Boniface was still alive at that time and, in his position as Archbishop of Mainz, performed the coronation of Pepin.

Three years later the new pope, Stephen II, was still in tense conflict with the Lombards. So he made the shrewd decision to travel to Paris and anoint Pepin, confirming the man's position as king. While he was there Stephen also anointed Pepin's twelve-year old son Charlemagne as an heir, and did the same for son Carloman who was three years of age. Among the Franks it was common for all sons to inherit part of their father's kingdom. And while there was no precedent for this kind of activity by a pope, it seemed like a good idea, and it bore fruit.

Pepin promised the pope that he would march against the Lombards and force them to agree that they would never attack Rome again. Further, he would make their king give up Ravenna and the lands that connected it to Rome. And once Pepin had possession of those properties, he would donate them in perpetuity to the pope.

With that done, Pepin marched south and made good on his promise, forcing Lombard king Aistulf to give the lands. Apparently Aistulf's word was not very good, however, for Pepin no sooner departed Italy than the Lombard king began to attack Rome again. This required Pepin to return two years later, in 756 AD, and force the physical handover of lands to the pope. As a penalty for the king's dishonorable behavior, additional lands were also ceded at this time. And the Lombard king was compelled to swear loyalty to Pepin.

These acts formally created the Papal States, which the popes would rule for more than a thousand years. This ownership made the religious leader a secular authority over lands which essentially constituted a small kingdom. Suddenly the pope found himself with real power as the head of this small country. And he became wealthy as well, with revenues from all these lands coming into his coffers.

The pope was emerging as a recognizable force in the world.

Twelve years later Pepin passed away and Charlemagne rose to become king of the Franks in 768 AD. He implemented changes that transformed Europe and brought it a step closer to the Crusades. At first he shared the substantial kingdom of the Franks with his brother Carloman. But his brother died three years after they were both crowned, so Charlemagne then ruled the entire empire by himself.

His attention was called to the south in 772 AD because the king of the Lombards was once again attacking cities in the Papal States. Pope Adrian I appealed to Charlemagne to give his support, as his father Pepin had done before him, and won a favorable response. Charlemagne came southward with his army and captured the Lombard king at Pavia in Northern Italy. He forced the man into a monastery, then placed the Iron Crown of the Lombards on his own head.

Arriving in Rome, Charlemagne gave back to the pope the cities that the Lombards had taken from him, and confirmed his father's gift of all the Papal States.

In return, the pope was happy to perform a service for Charlemagne, crowning two of the man's sons so they could rule over parts of the growing Frankish empire. Carloman was made king of Italy, changing his name to Pepin at the same time. Louis became king of Aquitaine in the southeastern corner of France, which extended to the border with the Moors.

It was Louis who led the attacks into the Spanish region known as Catalonia and its most prominent city of Barcelona. When Barcelona fell, it was a major step in the Reconquista—the long process of reconquering the Spanish lands lost to the Muslim conquest.

The Reconquista had its birth shortly after the Muslim armies first swept across the Iberian peninsula. The invaders discovered that the strip of mountains along the northern shore of Spain had become filled with Spanish Christians fleeing in that direction, so they came in pursuit. The local people made their stand in those mountains and turned back the Muslim forces, thereby founding the kingdom of Asturias. The first acknowledged king of that country, Alfonso I, more than doubled the size of Asturias in 740 AD when he conquered the land in the northwest corner of Spain known as Galicia. Fourteen years later he also captured the nearby fortified city of León.

Alfonso was able to accomplish all of this with his small army because many Berber soldiers from North Africa, who were part of the Arab army, became dissatisfied with their second-class treatment and abandoned the Arab Muslims. They had been stationed in Galicia and León, and willingly came over to Alfonso. Many of these Berbers converted to Christianity and continued to live in the northern lands where they were now welcomed.

In a strategic move, Alfonso urged all the people of León and the surrounding countryside to move northward as well, creating an unpopulated and barren borderland between his enlarged kingdom and the Muslims in the south. This empty buffer zone extended as far as the Douro River.

Those were the first steps of the Reconquista in the northwest. When Charlemagne's troops, led by his son, re-took Barcelona and the Catalan region in the northeast of Spain, the process of re-conquering the land was fully under way.

The knights-on-foot who were created by Charles Martel were now on horseback and the full flower of knighthood was on display. The credit for this is something so small that it is almost always overlooked. It was the invention of the stirrup. This simple device, attached to a saddle, allowed a man heavily encased in metal armor to stay on his horse. Without stirrups, any time the man leaned too far to one side or the other, the weight would pull him off his horse. And in battle, leaning to one side or the other with sword or ax in hand was a requirement. With the knight's

feet firmly placed in stirrups, he could also throw all his force behind each blow without worrying about keeping his balance.

Charlemagne has often been credited with the flowering of
knighthood in this way, though much of the credit should probably go to many hard-working blacksmiths. But he did make a
tremendous contribution by expanding his empire so much that
the only way his best soldiers could reasonably service it and re-
spond to emergencies was on horseback.

He ruled all of what is now France, plus part of Spain, Northern Italy, all of Belgium, the Netherlands and Switzerland, as well
as most of Germany, Austria and Slovenia, with parts of the Czech
Republic, Hungary and Croatia thrown in.

Without knights on horseback, winning that large an area—
and then ruling it—would have been virtually impossible. So he
invested heavily in his knights, and many of them were granted
lands in the territories he had won. That in turn contributed to the
growth of the feudal system in the Middle Ages.

The oldest surviving work in French literature preserves in
dramatic and romantic manner the story of Charlemagne's be-
loved knight, Roland. It was an epic poem simply titled *The Song
of Roland*. This valiant knight was ambushed accompanying Charlemagne back from a campaign into Spain and fought bravely
against his attackers, but was tragically slain. Many other epic
poems and stories about knights in shining armor would follow.

An epic event of a different kind was about to take place in
Rome, and it had its roots in a personal attack on the new pope,
Leo III. Some partisans had apparently supported a different can-
didate for pope, and physically attacked him in the streets of
Rome in 799 AD. When he appealed to Charlemagne for help, the
attackers leveled charges of adultery and perjury against Leo.
Charlemagne sided with the pope, and the attackers were exiled.

In gratitude, Leo crowned Charlemagne emperor of the Roman
Empire on Christmas Day in 800 AD. This was a monumental
moment for both the former king and the pope. Two of Charlemagne's sons were kings under him, so elevating him to emperor
and ruler of kings was a fitting step. It was also true, however,
that the Byzantine Empire in Constantinople had ruled continu-

Fig. 5   Mounted knights in the service of Charlemagne,
seen in a Medieval depiction of events in the Song of Roland

ously from the time the Roman emperors moved to that city, and had weakly but continuously tried to win back Rome and other parts of the original empire.

The pope's crowning of Charlemagne set aside the weak Byzantine claims of superiority over Rome and the Franks. And in fact by elevating Charlemagne as emperor of the *Roman Empire*, Leo asserted not only equality with the emperor in Constantinople but possibly superiority to the eastern empire. The Byzantine emperor was outraged. Charlemagne was pleased. And these events would have a strong effect on the Crusades when those campaigns were later stirred to life.

This was also one of the most important breakthrough moments in establishing the power of the pope and the Vatican. By crowning Charlemagne as emperor—the highest power in Europe and the ruler over kings—Leo also established the pope as a kingmaker. Obtaining the pope's blessing became a must-have for new kings and queens. And when there were multiple claimants to a throne, or a king wanted a divorce, or wanted moral support on any issue, it became common practice to seek the approval of the pope in resolving the matter. The accumulation of all these things made the pope a very powerful person.

It should be noted that addition to being a religious leader, the pope also ruled the Papal States, so he was no stranger to the exercise of political power. Some popes would wield this political power weakly, but others would use it very effectively to benefit their Church and increase the power of the Vatican.

Fig. 6   Charlemagne being crowned emperor by Pope Leo III

Chapter
4

The Holy Land
and Seeds of War

*C*he early Roman emperor Constantine lived only three hundred years after the birth of Christ but he had more to do with the Crusades than most people realize. The often-told story of his life is that his quest to become emperor was in desperate straits and he was in danger of being killed, when he had a vision of a Christian symbol—the Greek letters *chi* and *rho*.[12] He put that symbol on the shields of his soldiers, won the victory and lived. So he became the protector of Christians. The reality is a little more complex. Constantine's mother Helena was a devout Christian. This would have had a significant effect on him over the years, setting the stage for his epiphany on the battlefield and his willingness to be supportive of Christians.

Another of his contributions came about because the existing emperor against whom he was fighting had placed his new capital at Nicomedia, just east of the Bosphorus waterway in modern Turkey which separates Europe from Asia. When Constantine was crowned emperor, he moved the capital 62 miles west and placed it directly on the Bosphorus waterway at the ancient Greek city of Byzantium. That city was soon renamed in his honor as Constantinople.

Fig. 7 Helena, the mother of Constantine, in the Holy Land

With the power of the Roman empire now at Constantinople rather than Rome, it was not too surprising that invaders were ultimately able to sack Rome and destroy the empire in the West. But they were never able to sack Constantinople so the empire continued to flourish in the East.

That empire included the Holy Land, as well as much of the Middle East and North Africa. With Constantine's blessing, his devout mother Helena made a pilgrimage to the Holy Land where she set about finding and restoring many of the holy sites associated with the life of Jesus Christ. The most famous of these was the celebrated Church of the Holy Sepulchre which she directed be built on the site identified as the burial place of Jesus after his crucifixion.

It was these holy places, clearly marked and commemorated by Constantine's mother, that became the places to which Christian pilgrims traveled over all the years that followed. And it was the Muslim actions taken against those pilgrims that became the stated reason—or pretext in some views—for launching the Crusades.

The people of ancient Persia arose again at this time in what was known as the Sassanid Empire, and came west to attack the Byzantines. These invaders swept across all of the Middle East and Egypt before being pushed back again. By 628 AD the Byzantine emperors had essentially regained all the lands they had before, but had lost many soldiers and their resources were seriously depleted.

Then came Muhammad.

By the end of Muhammad's life in 632 AD he had fought many battles and converted all of Saudi Arabia to Islam. But he had not ventured out of the country. His successors felt no such limit and three years later set out on campaigns of conquest and conversion into the Sassanid Empire by attacking what is now called Iraq. At the same time, they plunged into the Byzantine Empire by attacking Damascus, Aleppo and Antioch in what is now Syria. Turning south, they took Lebanon and then Jerusalem. They continued onward to the Nile and seized what are now the cities of Cairo and Alexandria in Egypt.

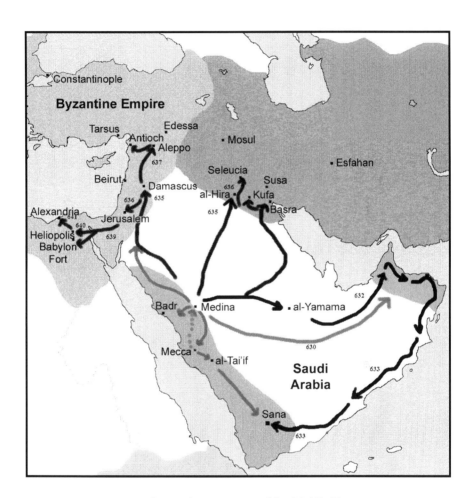

Fig. 8   Muslim conquest of the Middle East

Just like that, Muslim rule came to the Middle East. Large numbers of Christians still lived in these lands, but for many years the treatment they received was somewhere between harsh and fair. Christians were allowed to worship according to their faith, but only in approved churches. They were not allowed to attempt conversion of any Muslim. They had to wear specific clothing and give way to any Muslim on the street. But they were tolerated. And a limited number of pilgrims were allowed to come to the Holy Land each year.

But then harsher rulers came to power in the Muslim world. In 1009 the Egyptian Caliph al-Hakim bi-Amr Allah ordered the destruction of the Church of the Holy Sepulchre. Within a few years virtually all the churches and convents in Palestine were destroyed or confiscated. A generation passed before Christians were allowed to begin rebuilding the churches again.

But a greater danger was coming. The Seljuk Turks who lived on the northern edge of the Sassanid Empire near the Aral Sea had been converted to Islam, and now began moving southwest to create an empire of their own. By 1055 they had taken much of Persia and even captured Baghdad.

The Turks plunged into the Byzantine Empire in 1068, and established themselves in Western Anatolia—which is now called Turkey. After defeating the Byzantine forces in a major battle there,[13] the Seljuk Turks spread across all of central Anatolia, leaving the Byzantines with only isolated cities along the coast, including Constantinople. So at this point, most of the remaining Byzantine possessions were in Greece and the Balkan States.

At that same time, the Turks captured Jerusalem. Then, after a revolt, they were forced to besiege and take the city again. This second time they killed 3,000 of the rebels, who may have included Christians among them.

In 1081 the Byzantine emperor who would call for the Crusades ascended the Eastern throne. His name was Alexios I. At first he tried to push back the Turks from his territory using his own forces, but did not succeed. So Alexios stifled his pride and asked for help from Pope Urban II in 1095.

This request was a long-shot, because relations between the Eastern and Western empires had been going steadily downhill ever since Charlemagne was crowned emperor in the West by an earlier pope. This culminated in the Schism of 1054 over several religious issues, including whether the pope had universal jurisdiction over Christians. That schism divided all Christians between Roman Catholic and Eastern Orthodox—and this division has persisted to the present day.

So Alexios must have exhausted all other possible options to save his empire from the Turks, because he now tried to reach out to the pope in spite of that severely contentious schism.

Historians have concluded that Alexios only wanted some mercenary troops who would fight under his generals. He seemed to be as shocked as anyone when his appeal resulted in the Crusades. But there were deep forces at work that he did not realize—and which are still often overlooked today. We explore them here.

Spain's Reconquista and El Cid

In Spain, the Reconquista was still moving forward. After Barcelona and Catalonia were captured by Charlemagne's son Louis, the Basque people of northeastern Spain revolted against Muslim rule and created the small kingdom of Pamplona in 824 AD, which was later called Navarre. Around that same time, the small kingdom of Aragon was formed between Navarre and Catalonia. With that, all of Spain along the Pyrenees mountain range was recovered from the Muslim rulers.

The Reconquista was also becoming highly active in Northern Spain at this time. King Ordoño I of Asturias decided to repopulate some of the cities in the deserted buffer zone south of his kingdom. Among these was the fortress city of León, which was repopulated in 856 AD. This city would go on to be the capital of the kingdom of León and a major contributor to the Reconquista.

His successor, king Alfonso III, made a highly significant contribution by sending a nobleman named Vimara Peres to capture the land between the Minho and Douro Rivers on the Atlantic coast. This conquest included the city of Porto and the area that carried the old Roman name of Portus Cale—which was commonly called Portucale. As his reward, Peres was made lord over this

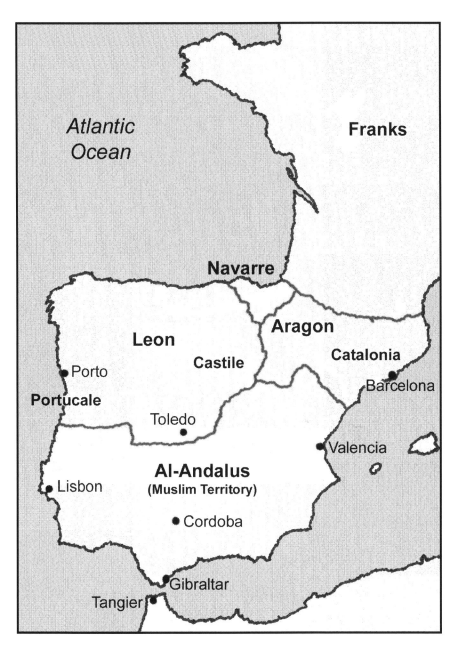

*Fig. 9 Map of the Spanish peninsula shows progress
of the Reconquista by 1085*

county of Portucale. Later, many additional sections of land would be added to the south, and this became the country known as Portugal.

A small county in the eastern part of Asturias began to make a name for itself a few years later. It was called Castile. In 882 AD the count of Castile began to repopulate another city in the buffer zone which was called Burgos. Burgos would eventually become the capital city of the kingdom of Castile. And that kingdom would be highly active in the Reconquista as well.

In 939 AD, when Ramiro II was king of León, Galicia and Asturias, he plunged south of the Douro River—which had marked the southern boundary of the buffer zone—and defeated the Muslim forces at Simancas. With this, the boundary of his realm was moved down to Salamanca on the Tormes River. By this time all three kingdoms were united under one king. And the lands of León had now grown so large with this expansion that it became customary to refer to the whole realm that he ruled as simply being the kingdom of León.

Within that kingdom, the county of Castile also extended its lands southward at this time. By doing so it became large enough that it embraced almost a quarter of the lands in León, and its Count began taking on many of the attributes of a king in his own right.

In 1064 Ferdinand I of León conquered the center part of Portugal as far as Coimbra on the Mondego River.

His son, Alfonso VI continued that work by winning battles against the small Muslim kingdoms across the middle of Spain and compelling them to pay annual tribute to the Christian kingdom of León. In one of those battles he took the city of Toledo in 1085. This was the old Christian capital of all Spain before the arrival of the Muslims, so it was an important psychological victory as well as a militarily important one. He managed to hold Toledo despite many attempts by Muslim armies to recover it.

At the same time, Alfonso captured a small town 46 miles north of Toledo that would come to be known as Madrid. In the years that followed, Madrid would eventually outstrip Toledo and all the other cities of Spain in size and prominence.

At first there was nothing particularly romantic about a person being a knight in those days. He was just a soldier wearing a heavy load of armor. On the field of battle, a mounted knight was like a modern-day tank—able to overrun infantry and deliver serious blows, while being well protected against most weapons.

But being a mounted knight was expensive, so this class of warrior tended to be limited to men from noble families who could afford the cost. That made knighthood respected. But it did not make knights loved. This was due to the simple fact that when battles were not being fought, knights were still in the service of their lords. So they were often called upon to obtain taxes from those who would not pay, or to fight against the lord's neighbors. This meant attacking and burning towns and cities as necessary to carry out the orders given to them. So most knights were respected and feared.

This changed dramatically with the arrival of a Spanish knight known as El Cid.

This man who brought reflected honor to all knights was born into a noble family of Castile as Rodrigo Diaz de Vivar. He received his military training in the court of Ferdinand I, who was the king of León and Count of Castile. When Ferdinand died in 1065, he divided his realm among his three sons, with Sancho receiving Castile. Rodrigo stayed with Sancho and served him well as commander of his troops.

The knightly Rodrigo extended Castile's lands southward by leading many victories against the Muslim armies. Yet he treated the defeated people honorably, earning from them the name al-Sayyid which meant The Lord. Soon his own soldiers were imitating them by calling him El Cid.

When fighting broke out among the three royal brothers, El Cid defended his master and defeated the other two, Alfonso of León and Garcia of Galicia. This re-united all three lands into one kingdom again. Unfortunately Sancho was killed by an assassin shortly thereafter, so the united kingdom fell to Alfonso.

Needless to say, the fact that El Cid had previously defeated Alfonso and driven him from his kingdom hung like a black cloud over the relationship between the two men. So despite El Cid's hero status, he was sent into exile.

Living in the borderlands between Christian and Muslim rulers, El Cid followed his conscience, sometimes leading troops against Muslims, sometimes leading troops against Christians. The only two things that remained constant were that he was almost universally victorious, and he won the respect of both sides.

King Alfonso kept El Cid at arm's length until a Muslim army defeated Alfonso's troops in 1086. Then the king was forced to eat crow and ask his hero to return. That was all it took to secure the Christian borders once again.

In fact, El Cid then had the liberty to pursue a personal project, the conquest of Valencia on the coast of the Mediterranean. He accomplished that feat in 1094, becoming master of that rich city and its surrounding lands. He lived there with his wife Jimena and their three children. And the admiration for him continued to grow into legends of chivalry and honor. [14]

Much later, wondrous tales of King Arthur's court and his glorious knights would be written by Geoffrey of Monmouth and Chrétien de Troyes. But it is significant to note that those writings came only after the Knights Templar were created and set a new standard for knightly behavior. Until then, the world was still much in need of knights who answered to a higher calling.

The visibility of the Reconquista to the rest of Europe was demonstrated by the fact that King Alfonso also received the help of two highly capable knights from the Burgundy region of France. In return he offered them the best inducement he could imagine: marriage to his two daughters and entry into the royal family. The rich prize won by these two knights for joining the fight against Muslim occupation made their stories strikingly attractive to people in Europe, if not quite as exciting as that of El Cid.

The rest of Europe had also changed in the days after Charlemagne. His vast empire that spanned most of the continent was divided among his three grandsons, essentially forming France in the west, Germany in the east, and a middle kingdom running from the Netherlands to Italy.

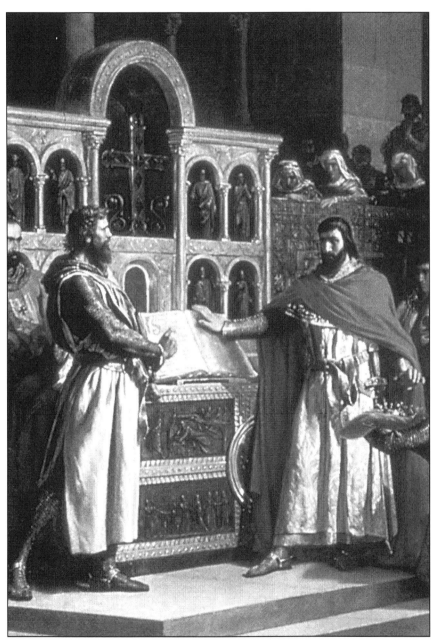

Fig. 10   El Cid, on the left, hears King Alfonso swear that he was not reponsible for the assassination of the former king.

Europe splintered further into many pieces and internal wars resulted until Otto I of Germany expanded his kingdom by taking over the territory from the Netherlands to Italy. Following Charlemagne's example, Otto then went to Rome in 962 AD and was crowned Holy Roman Emperor. This began a curious love-hate relationship between the emperor and the pope. Otto strengthened the role of clerics in his empire, which was much appreciated. But at the same time he sought to establish his authority over the pope, which was deeply resented.

Otto's descendants followed him in the role of emperor, lending some stability to Europe. And they continued the close, though sometimes difficult, ties to the pope.

Finally a pope with real backbone, Leo IX, was chosen in the city of Worms, Germany, at an assembly of church leaders convened by the emperor in 1048. However he would not accept the honor unless it was approved by the clergy and people of Rome, as in times past. So he went to Rome, won that approval, and became the new pope.

That was only the first sign of the reforms he wanted to implement. And these were reforms only in the sense of going back to the simpler and possibly purer practices of Christianity's earlier years. He even convened synods of church officials to discuss rooting out the practice of simony, in which forgiveness or religious offices were sold for money. If he was not successful, at least he worked at it.

Among the many shifting borders of countries at this time, there was one change that was particularly significant. William the Conqueror, Duke of Normandy, conquered England in 1066. This created a new dynasty that would be important not only for Great Britain but also for the Crusades and the Knights Templar.

When Gregory VII became pope, he went beyond Leo in asserting that the German emperor could not create priests nor determine who would be pope. To establish his point, he excommunicated emperor Henry IV three times, and eventually the pope prevailed. This significantly increased the power of the papacy. Gregory also vigorously attacked the practice of simony, which was an ongoing problem.

It is a little-known fact that Gregory was the first pope to call for Crusades to the Holy Land. The Byzantine Empire's defeat at the Battle of Manzikert in 1071 happened just before Gregory was chosen as pope, and he responded by urging a Western military campaign against the Muslims. Unfortunately his ongoing confrontations with the European emperor made such cooperation politically impossible.

Pope Urban II continued the reforms of Gregory, but in a much more diplomatic manner. This made it possible for him to issue the call for a Crusade after he received an appeal from Byzantine emperor Alexios I in 1095. And the forces of Christendom began to assemble.

The First Crusade
and Pope Urban II

It is widely known that when representatives from Alexios came to him at Piacenza in Northern Italy, Urban II was very much taken with the idea of a military force being assembled under papal leadership. If he was not so excited about helping the Eastern Orthodox Church, which had split off from his own church, then at least this would put him at a slightly superior position to his rivals.

When the pope floated this idea at a council of church leaders and local nobility in Clermont later in 1095, there was a surprisingly strong response from his audience. So he began to energetically preach a crusade in letters and speeches. He was supported by other church and social leaders who did the same. Their stated goal was to free the Holy Land and Christian churches from the Muslim Turks. There was little or no mention of coming to the aid of the Byzantine Empire, which was the Eastern emperor's true purpose.

In return, those who went on this quest were promised the remission of their sins. That would be a good thing to have, of course. But one could also gain remission of sins by confession to a priest and receiving an indulgence. Or, as could be done in those

Fig. 11   Peter the Hermit preaching the People's Crusade

days, a simple payment to a priest could get you remission of your sins. So why would you go on a military campaign and probably die in order to get that forgiveness? This has been one of the enduring mysteries of the Crusades.

That was where Europe's experience with Spain and the Reconquista came in. After the Muslim invaders had spread over almost all of the Spanish peninsula in a few years, there had been a long and steady march in the other direction. Christians had pushed the Muslims back consistently, and now had regained half of the peninsula. That they would keep on marching and winning was not in doubt.

When faced with an exhortation to recapture the Holy Land, Europeans did not see Christian-Muslim conflict as a distant thing. They had seen it on their own doorstep. And their long experience with the Reconquista established the belief that Christians would *always* prevail over Muslim forces—and that Muslim lands would become Christian lands again. To them, victory in the Holy Land was virtually guaranteed.

They were not going off to battle in the Holy Land, they were going for certain victory. They were going so they could be among the celebrants in Jerusalem. And they would get remission of their sins as well.

Nothing showed this more clearly than the first thing that happened in the Crusades. Even before the military leaders could pull together a proper crusade, a People's Crusade was formed. Up to 80,000 common people, with a few lower-level knights among them, were persuaded that marching to the Holy Land would be a walk to glory. A priest named Peter the Hermit led most of them forward in April of 1096. Others came of their own volition about that same time.

After many confrontations this mass of people finally arrived in Constantinople and the emperor was appalled. This exceedingly large assembly of bedraggled humanity was definitely not the small force of disciplined fighting men he had hoped to receive. So he sent them onward into the nearby lands controlled by the Seljuk Turks, where almost all of them were quickly killed.

That was how powerful the golden image of the Reconquista was in Europe at that time. The certainty of Christian victory

Fig. 12   The leaders of the Princes' Crusade

spurred an outpouring of people that surprised everyone involved.

Four months after that unruly mass of people set out, the official expedition began. This would be called the Princes' Crusade, because the younger brothers or sons of Europe's kings led the various detachments of soldiers who arrived for this campaign. Apparently the kings themselves were being cautioned not to go, because their death in battle could cause wars of succession that would upset the fragile balance of power in Europe. Their relatives, however, were eager to go.

The ranks of this campaign once again swelled with common soldiers caught up by the seemingly guaranteed victory, but it is not so clear that their leaders were likewise blinded by that vision. Almost all of these leaders were knights, but unfortunately knighthood was not generally in good repute during these times, as we saw earlier. The constant warfare across Europe had knights prominently on display among the destruction wrought in the countryside. This did not leave the best of impressions on the local populace.

In contrast with that image were the glowing tales and legends of El Cid spreading across Europe. His reputation in Spain was almost that of a living saint. At the time that the Crusade was being preached across Europe, El Cid had done the almost-impossible by taking the city of Valencia from its Muslim owners and now ruled the city by himself.

If the other knights of Europe missed the subtlety of his fair treatment of all the people under his authority, they at least saw the bright, almost blinding example of a knight who fought for Christianity against the Muslims—and was rewarded with honors beyond imagining. And at the end of his efforts he ruled a small realm of his own, carved out of Muslim land.

So the princes and knights of Europe had an enticing dream of their own which added significantly to their motivation to join this Crusade. It may have been a different dream than that of the common man, but it was no less compelling.

There were four main leaders of the Princes' Crusade who essentially amassed four separate armies which alternately cooperated and competed with each other during this long campaign.

Godfrey of Bouillon was the Duke of Lower Lorraine and drew men to his standard from all across the lands that are today Northeastern France and Belgium. He was strengthened in his crusading role because his capable brothers Baldwin and Eustace went with him and made their own strong contributions.

Hugh of Vermandois was the younger brother of the king of France, Philip I, and drew his army from central and Northwestern France. Included in his contingent was Robert Curthose, who was not only Duke of Normandy but the brother of King William II of England.

Raymond IV, the Count of Toulouse, gathered his knights and soldiers from Southern France and the borderlands of Spain. The pope's representative for this crusade, Bishop Adhemar of Le Puy, traveled with Raymond on these campaigns. The Count of Barcelona, Berenguer Ramon II, was also part of this contingent.

Bohemond, the Prince of Taranto, ruled the southeastern part of Italy. He brought a force from the Italian peninsula that included his nephew Tancred, who would distinguish himself in battle.

Now the Crusades could begin in earnest.

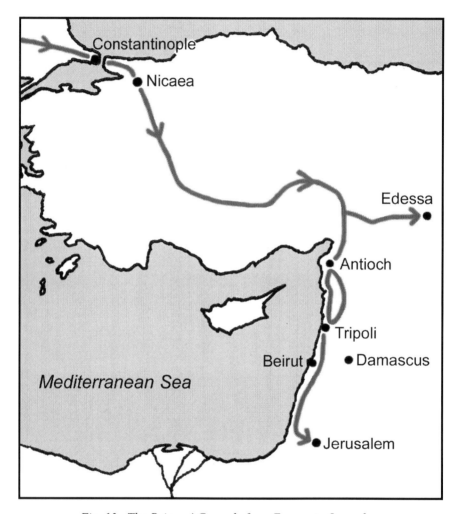

Fig. 13   The Princes' Crusade from Europe to Jerusalem

On the Road to
Jerusalem

$\mathcal{T}$he four armies of the First Crusade set out for the Holy Land in August of 1096, taking different paths. By agreement, they met at Constantinople, and were finally together by spring of the following year. The Byzantine emperor was once again distraught by the sea of soldiers who assembled on his doorstep. Clearly these were more people than he felt he could control, so he withheld food and supplies to them for their campaign until they swore to give any conquered land to him.

Having resolved that detail, the Crusaders set out for the capital city of the Turks in Anatolia which we now know as Turkey. That city was Nicaea, only 56 miles southeast of Constantinople. Due to its importance, the city was fiercely contested and a siege was required. But even so, it fell to the Crusaders within two months. The Byzantine emperor's representatives enforced their agreement by taking control of the city and forbidding any looting by the Crusaders. To compensate for those actions, the emperor made certain the European troops were richly rewarded.

With a satisfying victory under their belts, the Crusaders pressed onward. And though they made steady progress, they were harassed by the regional sultan, Kilij Arslan I, who fought them in pitched battle on July 1, 1097 before retreating. But the local leader did not leave them in peace, destroying the sources of food and water in front of them so that the Crusaders were tormented by hunger and thirst as they continued southeast across Anatolia.

The sweeping stories of battles fought on the Crusades, and the thousands who died, can make us forget that the life of each person on the crusade was valuable and the loss of each of them could be a tragedy. So we take a moment to consider the ordeal of Sweyn and his wife Florine on the Princes' Crusade.

Sweyn was a younger son of Sweyn II, the king of Denmark. Florine was the daughter of Odo I, the Duke of Burgundy.[15] They could have lived an enchanted life in the comfort of Europe. But for whatever reason, they decided to go on crusade to the Holy Land. And brought 1500 soldiers with them.

While crossing the middle of Anatolia, the different armies and militias sometimes split off in search of food or to find the safest way forward. We are told that when the small force led by Sweyn and Florine was alone, they were attacked by a larger army of Turks. All day they fought, with the number of European soldiers constantly being whittled down. Florine was pierced by arrows, but continued to fight at her husband's side. In desperation they plunged into the ranks of the Turks, trying to open an escape route, but were overcome in the attempt. They died together on that foreign field.

Perhaps these moments of their life are worth remembering—otherwise they are lost among so many others.

Shortly thereafter, the surviving Christian armies reached the northern edge of the Holy Land and began to move southward along the Mediterranean coast toward the great city of Antioch. There they began an arduous siege and the battle for the Holy Land began in earnest.

It was at this time that a personal tragedy reshaped the crusade. Baldwin, the brother of Godfrey of Bouillon, had gone off by himself with a small party of men because he was devastated by the death of his wife. In addition to this personal loss, her lands had been the source of his support in Europe, so that was lost as well. Having no reason to ever return to Europe, Baldwin took his

Fig. 14   Florine of Burgundy, on the First Crusade

small force and captured a fortified town northeast of Antioch, resolving to make that his new home.

But a few months later he received an intriguing offer from Thoros, the Armenian leader of the nearby city of Edessa. The man had rebelled against his Muslim rulers was in desperately need of help. He had appealed to the Crusader armies at Antioch, but they were struggling to maintain their siege and gave him no aid. So Baldwin was asked to come with his men and help Edessa.

Baldwin gladly accepted this opportunity and established himself in the city, fighting to protect it. When Thoros died on March 9 of 1098, Baldwin became the first Count of Edessa. Following in the footsteps of El Cid, he had led Christian soldiers against Muslim occupiers, and won a marvelous city-state for himself.

The effect on the other Crusaders was electric. But not necessarily in a good way. When Antioch finally fell to the Crusaders in June of that year, Bohemond of Taranto and Raymond of Toulouse both claimed to be the ruler of the city. To decide the matter, an appeal was made to Alexios I in Constantinople to see if he wanted to claim the city as provided in their prior agreement. When the emperor declined to send troops to stake that claim, the Crusaders declared that he had abandoned all claims to recovered cities in the Holy Land and moved on. An appeal to the pope in Rome also failed to resolve the dispute. Finally, in early 1099, Raymond saved the stalled crusade by yielding to Bohemond, who became the first Prince of Antioch.

With two Crusader states having been established behind them, the rest of the Crusaders pushed onward to Jerusalem. They briefly began to besiege the city of Arqa near Tripoli, then broke off when the Muslim Emir of Tripoli invited them into the city and gave them fresh supplies. So the Crusaders left him in peace and plunged straight through to Jerusalem without wasting any more time attacking cities in between. They arrived in front of the walls of the holy city on June 7, 1099.

After such a long and arduous journey to this place which had taken years, the assault on Jerusalem passed relatively quickly. An initial attack failed. But when word came that a large Muslim force had left Egypt to relieve the city, a desperate and determined

Fig. 15   Baldwin entering Edessa

attack was launched. By July 15 the Crusaders had penetrated the walls and the defenders were routed. By all accounts there was a horrific massacre of the Muslims and Jews in the city that day. And when the dust had settled, Jerusalem was in Christian hands once more.

The majority of all the Crusaders heaved a sigh of relief, packed their bags, and began to board ships so they could return to Europe and be with their families again.

A few knights stayed in the Holy Land to protect the Christian pilgrims who now began to arrive in greater numbers. Among those knights was a young man named Hugh de Payens. As historian Charles Addison noted, Hugh "had fought with great credit and renown at the siege of Jerusalem."[16] Although few would have remarked on him at the time, Hugh would eventually call together eight other knights and kneel with them on Temple Mount in Jerusalem to form the Knights Templar. When those knights in turn acknowledged him as their first Grand Master, the glorious, secretive and controversial history of their unique brotherhood began.

Two Remarkable Young Men Named Hugh

Hugh de Payens was born into an aristocratic family in the large county of Champagne just east of Paris. He was surrounded by the fertile countryside whose vineyards produced the sparkling wine of that same name. Hugh was heir to the lands of Payns, a town situated just seven miles from Troyes, the capital city of Champagne. And he was trained as a knight—obligated to fight in the service of the powerful Count who lived there.

A major event happened in 1093, when Hugh was twenty-three years of age. The lord of Champagne died, and the man's brother—four years younger than de Payens—became the Count of Champagne. By chance, the young Count's name was also Hugh, and they had known each other for as long as they could remember because they were both members of the local aristocracy and lived within walking distance of each other's home. They developed a close bond between them which would continue for the rest of their lives and affect the course of history.

The nineteen-year-old Count of Champagne ruled one of the largest land areas in France, and faced the daunting task of taking his place in French society at a level only one step below that of the king of France, to whom he pledged his loyalty. Having a

*Fig. 16 The cathedral in Troyes, where a religious council was held
as an essential step in forming the Knights Templar*

trusted advisor such as the slightly older Hugh de Payens would have been a great comfort to him.

Three years later, when armies began massing for the Crusades, Hugh de Champagne[17] was apparently among those deemed too valuable to the stability of the country to join the holy warriors and did not lead a force into the campaign. But there was no such restraint on Hugh de Payens, who was a capable knight and ready to serve.

Champagne was located close to the duchy of Lorraine where Godfrey of Bouillon was assembling his large army for the crusade. So while there was no specific record of where Hugh de Payens served in the First Crusade, it would have been reasonable for him to have served in this neighbor's force. That deduction is enhanced by the mutually-supportive relationship Hugh later shared with Godfrey's cousin Baldwin II in the Holy Land.

After the arduous Princes' Crusade wound its way to Jerusalem and that city fell, Godfrey of Bouillon became its first ruler. This put Godfrey's knights in an advantageous position, and may well have influenced their decision to stay in the Holy Land when so many other Europeans went home. Hugh was among the knights who stayed.

When Godfrey died in 1100, he was succeeded by his brother Baldwin as king of Jerusalem. Hugh and the other knights simply continued as before, fighting skirmishes with the local Muslim militias who attacked the visiting pilgrims from time to time.

A completely different service to the stream of European visitors was provided by a group of local brothers in Jerusalem who maintained a hospital and cared for sick and weary pilgrims. These were the Hospitallers. They were a group of Benedictine monks attached to the monastery of Saint John.

When a man named Gerard Thom became provost of this group he organized them into a formal religious order and immediately began to solicit rich grants of property to support his order's much-needed work. The highest validation of his group's efforts came in 1113, when Pope Paschal II formally recognized it as the Order of Saint John of Jerusalem. They were officially assigned the black robe of the Benedictines, with a white cross added. It is important to note that they had no military role at that time. They were only monks providing shelter and medical care.

Hugh de Champagne became more active in these events in 1104 when he barely survived an assassination attempt in France. It caused him to contemplate his mortality and consider living a more religious life.[18] So he undertook his own journey to Jerusalem to be with his old friend Hugh de Payens. Since no European kings had gone on crusade by this time, de Champagne was one of the highest-ranking nobles to come to the Holy Land. His presence must have drawn a considerable amount of attention.

While there, de Champagne lived the difficult but satisfying life of a knight, faced with the hardships of military skirmishes and Spartan lifestyle. It also gave him a chance to renew his relationship with Baldwin, who was now king of Jerusalem, and had been one of his neighbors before the wars began.

In 1107 de Champagne returned to France to attend to the affairs of his province. His friend Hugh de Payens either accompanied him or followed shortly thereafter, because documents have been found in Champagne during the years leading up to 1113 that seem to have the signature of de Payens on them as a witness.

Once home in France, de Champagne became an active supporter of the works being done by Cistercian monks, and even contemplated taking religious vows himself. Since this would play such a central role in the formation of the Knights Templar and their subsequent life, it is worth taking a look at the source and popularity of these religious brotherhoods across Europe and the Middle East.

Christian monasteries were first formed in the Holy Land by disciples who wanted to live close to one of the charismatic holy men in the early days of Christianity and learn from that man. This led to the disciples forming small communities of people and constructing buildings in which to live. These eventually became recognized as monasteries. Some of these were large, while others were quite small. Some lasted for generations, with new holy men taking the lead, while others disappeared quickly for one reason or another.

Fig. 17   The Benedictine abbey at Monte Cassino

In the West, this way of life was adopted by Benedict of Nursia in Italy, who built his first monastery in 529 AD at Monte Cassino. This was a mountainous area located midway between Rome and Naples. In time, many more of his Benedictine monasteries were founded and they thrived in most major cities of Italy, Spain, France and England—as well as in many isolated places across Europe. The brothers of the Benedictine order were usually recognized by the black robes they wore.

The abbeys and monasteries they created were independent communities, and were not controlled by the pope in Rome. For the most part the members of these monasteries were lay brothers who simply studied, prayed and worked to support their monastery. They grew their own food and made basic products such as bread, wine and leather goods that could be sold in marketplaces. Whatever excess they gained that was more than they needed for their sustenance was given away as charity. The few who were ordained as priests would conduct the religious services attended by all the other brothers.

Then in 1098 a new order of monks was formed who called themselves Cistercians. They were driven by the belief that many of the Benedictine monasteries had drifted away from the original rules set by Saint Benedict for living an austere and holy life. So they began to revive those original rules in their own monasteries. To distinguish themselves from the Benedictines, the Cistercians wore white robes.

When the Knights Templar formed in 1119, they adopted many of the rules of these Cistercian monks. They also clothed themselves in white robes—then later added the red Templar cross to identify themselves. The reason for their connection to the Cistercians was quite fascinating. But a few other things had to happen first.

Founding of the Templars, and Saint Bernard

𝔄 remarkable series of events began to happen in 1114 when Hugh de Champagne returned to the Holy Land. He was accompanied by de Payens and possibly several other knights from their French province.

While he was there, de Champagne followed up on his heightened religious interest by making a grant of lands to the Cistercian Order. This allowed a young monk named Bernard to start a new monastery at Clairvaux just east of Troyes. The new abbot would eventually become known as St. Bernard.[19] He also would play a critical role in the rise of the Knights Templar, a moment that was drawing ever closer.

Then in 1116 the Count of Champagne left the affairs of Jerusalem in the hands of de Payens and returned to France.

Three years later a particularly bloody massacre of Christian pilgrims demonstrated clearly that a much stronger organization of knights was needed to protect these vulnerable people. It happened during Easter observances, when approximately seven hundred pilgrims from several countries set out on the mountainous road from Jerusalem to the Jordan River where Jesus had been baptized. While they were passing through a particularly desolate

Fig. 18   Saint Bernard of Clairvaux

area, Muslim raiders attacked suddenly and killed three hundred of them. Sixty more were taken captive. A few survivors managed to escape and return to Jerusalem, but by the time the Christian king of that city sent a party of knights to pursue the attackers, the marauders had already escaped.[20]

In response to these killings, and others across the Holy Land, Hugh de Payens called eight other knights to kneel with him on Temple Mount in Jerusalem and take a solemn obligation. They pledged to do everything within their power to safeguard the pilgrims who traveled to Jerusalem and other holy sites. They had no way of knowing the full implication of what they were doing—because their sworn oaths marked the creation of the Knights Templar.[21]

When Hugh met with the king of Jerusalem to tell him of the oaths he and his men had taken, the monarch was overjoyed. The beleaguered ruler had been king for only a year, and it had been a very difficult year. Since he was the cousin of the two previous rulers, Godfrey and Baldwin, he could at least count on the same supporters as the previous kings, and those supporters in turn kept their influence in court. So the man had styled himself as Baldwin II, and now gratefully received this pledge of greater service from de Payens. This arrangement was believed to have been confirmed by an assembly at Nablus in January of 1120.[22]

The king showed his appreciation by giving Hugh and his knights a wing of his palace on Temple Mount. There the Templars established their residences and meeting place. This building had previously served as the Al Aqsa Mosque and therefore was a grand and ornate structure. But the king was in the process of building a true palace for himself near the Tower of David in the city, so he soon gave the Templars the whole of his old palace on Temple Mount.

Since the Temple of Solomon had once stood on this Mount—which was now the knights' home and base of operations—they quickly became accepted everywhere as the Knights Templar.

Officially, the pope would later bestow on them the formal name *Pauperes commilitones Christi Templique Solomonici*. That is to say, the Poor Fellow-Soldiers of Christ and the Temple of Solomon. But to everyone, they were simply Templars.

*Fig. 19   The Templars built these arches on the front of Al Aqsa Mosque
when they used it as their headquarters*

The reference to poverty reflected the other vows taken by these knights, in addition to their promise to protect pilgrims. They swore to be more holy in their manner than many of their rough fellow Crusaders. To that end, Hugh and the other Templars took vows of poverty, chastity, and obedience. Their first oaths of obedience were given to Patriarch Warmund, the spiritual leader of Jerusalem, and to King Baldwin, the civil leader. In taking these vows, the Knights Templar assumed the lives of monks, just as one might find in an abbey or monastery. But instead of remaining isolated behind abbey walls their mission required them to be active in the world with sword in hand, fighting against any who attacked Christians in the Holy Land.

The other men who joined de Payens in this original circle of Knights Templar were Godfrey de Saint-Omer,[23] Payen de Montdidier, Andre de Montbard[24], Archambaud de St. Agnan, Geoffrey Bison, two men known only as Rossal and Gondamer, and a ninth knight who was not named. Only a few details about these men are known, with one of the most interesting facts being that they all lived in or near the province of Champagne before coming to the Holy Land. This seemed to be a close group of men whom Hugh de Payens came to know well, and whom he trusted.

At first they wore simple, unadorned clothing along with their armor when they went out on patrol. But in time they came to be recognized on the field of battle by the white robes they wore, surmounted by a large red cross. Given the support they received from St. Bernard, and the devoted interest in the Cistercians by their sponsor Hugh de Champagne, this was a natural choice of garment for them to wear. This was also the distinctive image by which they came to be known in the imaginations of people all over Europe and the East.

As we have seen, most knights in those days were admired for their power, but also feared because that power was often used to enrich themselves at the expense of others. All the knights who went to the Holy Land were accorded some measure of respect in Europe. But these knights who took vows of poverty, chastity, and obedience to God were raised to a higher level. Their vows did not allow them to enrich themselves personally. Nor could they establish a dynasty for their heirs, as others had done across the continent. These men used their formidable power only in the service of pilgrims and God. This endeared them to lords and commons alike.

The Templars soon began to have an impact on battles all across the Holy Land.

It is also said that imitation is the sincerest form of flattery. If so, the Hospitallers now paid the Templars the ultimate compliment. After Gerard Thom, the founder of the Hospitallers, died in 1120 his order of monks elected Raymond du Puy as their new leader. Du Puy was a knight, and saw the honors bestowed on the Knights Templar when they were formed the previous year. So he decided to add a knightly dimension to his own monastic order. He recruited a number of knights and created a separate group in the Hospitallers, to serve alongside the monks who still provided shelter and care for pilgrims.

Du Puy and his knights then took to the battlefields of the Holy Land with their armor covered by black robes marked with a white cross. They fought beside—and sometimes in rivalry with— the Knights Templar, whose shining armor was covered by white robes and a bright red cross.

Secret Passageways,
Secret Powers

After King Baldwin moved to his new palace near the Tower of David in the western part of Jerusalem, the Templars had sole possession of their massive headquarters. This strongly motivated them to "secure their perimeter" by carefully searching all the buildings and passageways on or under Temple Mount. While they were doing this, many legends tell us the knights acquired secrets and powers that enabled them to quickly rise to a position of tremendous authority and wealth.

Traditionally these secrets and powers have been attributed to discoveries involving Solomon's Temple, and they covered a wide range of possibilities. The Holy Grail, a miraculous cup said to have held the blood of Jesus and possessed of tremendous powers, was described in many legends. These included King Arthur and the Knights of the Round Table—which sometimes are interpreted as being based on the Knights Templar and their round churches.

One of the dark secrets suggested in the book *Holy Blood, Holy Grail* in 1982, and made popular by *The Da Vinci Code,* was that the Templars discovered and protected the bloodline of Jesus Christ, who was thought to have fathered a child by Mary Magdalene.

Fig. 20   The Holy Grail

This reportedly began a dynasty of secret descendants of Jesus, with serious repercussions for the Catholic Church.

Other explanations for the Templars' quick rise to power included discoveries involving the Ark of the Covenant, Hebrew religious writings containing mysteries such as Kabbalah, encrypted number systems allowing secret messages to be interpreted from the Bible, or the stone tablets of Moses which contained the sacred writing of God and transmitted divine power. All of these possibilities have their advocates, and in some cases the arguments presented on their behalf have been quite compelling.

If the Ark of the Covenant or the tablets of Moses were recovered, we would only know this if they eventually appeared in a private or public collection. That has not happened, so we are still awaiting conclusive proof that these objects were the valuables from Solomon's Temple found by the Knights Templar.

As to the Hebrew religious writings and mystical number systems, however, something intriguing has appeared, and that is the practice of Kabbalah. Arcane Kabbalah knowledge is thought to have been part of the original oral law of Judaism given to Moses by God on Mount Sinai around the 13th century BC, though some traditions assert that it goes back to Adam in the Garden of Eden. In any event, by the time of Solomon the mysteries of Kabbalah were said to have been openly and widely practiced. Then as more foreign conquests happened in Israel and Judah—leading up to and including the Babylonian Captivity—there was thought to be a great deal of concern that this esoteric knowledge would fall into the wrong hands. So the teachings of Kabbalah became tightly-held secrets shared with only a few, and virtually disappeared from sight.

Kabbalah was next seen being taught after the temple was destroyed for the last time in 70 AD. The teachings of Rabbi Shim'on son of Yohai were particularly prominent around that time. This special knowledge included a way to study the books that came to appear in the Old Testament, using methodologies which were clearly mystical in nature.

So here we have Hebrew religious teachings being practiced in the time of Solomon, then disappearing into secrecy, only to reappear after the temple fell. Of all the things that were rolled up and

Fig. 21 Ark of the Covenant

stored among the temple's most valuable possessions—and might be understood to confer special powers or abilities to its possessor—Kabbalah would have to be considered a serious candidate to be among them.

Since the Templars were later accused of following mystical Eastern practices, that only adds to the evidence pointing in this direction.

But did these secret underground passageways actually exist in Temple Mount, through which these things could be obtained? The answer is clearly "yes," since I have been in some of them myself.

A number of entry points into the underground corridors can still be seen today. Stairs in front of Al Aqsa Mosque go down into the Mount, as seen in Figure 19, where a boy stands at the top of the steps. What easier access could there possibly have been for the Templars who were using that building as their residence and headquarters?

Other stairs go down into the Mount at the place historically known as Solomon's Stables, but which now is the site of the El-Marwani underground mosque. In the 1860s and 1870s Charles Warren and Charles Wilson extensively mapped the hidden passageways, cisterns and rooms under the Mount, and others have added to their findings during the rare times that excavations have been permitted.

The collections of maps, photos and drawings from those excavations show that the stairway in front of Al Aqsa goes deep below the mosque and emerges at the large double-gate at the foot of the Mount's southern wall. Elevation maps show these steps followed the downward slope of the hillside before King Herod greatly expanded Temple Mount. Given that Al Aqsa Mosque was later built on this platform created by Herod, it could not have been the site of Solomon's Temple, which was built on the ground.

Although there have been differences of opinion in the past, it now seems clear that Solomon's Temple actually stood on the part of the Mount currently occupied by the Dome of the Rock. I went to Temple Mount and was able to gain access to an underground chamber that was immediately below where the Holy of Holies had been in the Temple. An ancient hole pierced the rock there, large enough to move valuables such as the contents of the Ark of the Covenant into the chamber secreted below in times of danger. Since I was able to get there, and the pierced rock was described in antiquity, it is almost certain that the Templars were able to get there. The only real question is: what was there for them to find?

Different people have suggested that the Grail, Ark, Kabbalah and many other things were there which gave the Templars tremendous power and enabled them to force the pope to give them special authority and privileges. The many books written on these subjects are too lengthy to be reproduced here, so they will have to stand on their own.

But the Templars definitely had other special advantages propelling them forward, and those are worth a look.

Hugh, Count of Champagne

In the year 1125 the Count of Champagne did a most extraordinary thing. He made his commitment to the Knights Templar complete. This was done by turning over all his lands and power to a distant relative. Then he came to Jerusalem again, and this time placed his hands in those of his lifelong friend, Grand Master Hugh de Payens.

By doing this, the Count agreed to serve the rest of his life as a Templar. And though he no longer personally appeared on the world stage, the newly-raised Templar knight who became known as Sir Hugh continued to work behind the scenes during a critical time for the young Templars. In order for them to be more than a minor cult of knights in Jerusalem, they needed to obtain the pope's approval of their order. They also needed to seek from the nobility of Europe the heavy financial support needed for their efforts.

Traditional accounts about the Templars say that King Baldwin of Jerusalem decided one day in 1126 to send a request to the influential Saint Bernard, Abbot of Clairvaux, asking the abbot to seek the pope's blessing for the Knights Templar. Bernard was

Fig. 22   Abbey of Saint Bernard at Clairvaux

then said to have accepted this mission, and things progressed from there.

The reality, as we have seen, was quite different. The saintly Bernard had received his lands and his monastery at Clairvaux from the hands of the Count of Champagne. For this, Bernard owed him a profound debt of gratitude. This was confirmed in a letter Bernard wrote to the Count on the occasion of Hugh's leaving France to become a Templar. This letter avowed the deep thanks Bernard owed to his benefactor.[25]

There was never any doubt that Bernard would be a passionate advocate for the Templars whenever Hugh de Champagne desired it. The request for Bernard's support clearly came from Sir Hugh and Grand Master de Payens—with King Baldwin signing a formal letter to give the request appropriate weight when Bernard approached the pope.

Bernard went to work immediately and arranged for Pope Honorius II to grant an audience with Hugh de Payens and four of his brother knights. With the pontiff's invitation in hand, de Payens set out for Rome in 1127. The pope received him and warmly approved the cause of the Knights Templar, then let his opinion be known.[26] He also summoned a great Council of the church to be held the following year in the city of Troyes. At that time the Templars' elevation to a formal Order of the Church would be discussed and offered for approval.

In case the hand of the former Count was not entirely obvious in these proceedings, it is noted that Troyes was the Count's family seat in Champagne.

Now that the critical council meeting had been arranged, de Payens had to move quickly. He desperately needed to recruit more knights into the Templars for two essential reasons. If he wanted the Knights Templar to be taken seriously as a substantial group, worthy of being made a formal monastic order, he needed to come before the Council with more than the nine-to-thirty knights variously estimated to be in his chivalric brotherhood at that time.

Equally important, he needed to put more knights into the field in the Holy Land against the overwhelming Muslim forces—not just to achieve victories, but to survive. This recruitment was one of his most pressing needs and—as a leader of knights—he was highly qualified to assess, inspire and enlist these people.

But he had another pressing need as well. And without it the service of these knights would be rendered virtually useless. He needed rich gifts from the kings and nobility of Europe to support and equip those knights, along with their sergeants, in the Holy Land. More than gold and silver, he needed lands and estates. Gold could be spent only once. But land and estates could be farmed to produce revenues year after year—and those streams of revenue could be spent forever. Unfortunately, fundraising was an area Hugh de Payens was ill equipped to handle.

His lands and manor of Payns had come to him by right as his father's son. He had no need to seek it, negotiate rights, define boundaries, or draw new contracts with local peasants who would farm the land and pay appropriate rents. Moreover, begging for gifts of land was beneath the dignity of a member of French nobility. Not that such begging was not done, but disrepute often fell upon those who did it.

De Payens lacked experience in determining the right amount to seek from a prospective donor, and how to tender the request properly to obtain a good response. Fortunately, he had people with him who were masters at this enterprise: the Christian brothers he had recruited in Lebanon.

These Lebanese brothers were descended from the Phoenicians of antiquity who were widely regarded as masters of sea trade, languages and business in the Mediterranean world. These skills were so deeply entrenched in their society that even in 1975 the average Lebanese person spoke three languages and Beirut was still the financial capital of the Middle East—until regional wars devastated the city.

But the land in which the Lebanese people lived was also marked by two indelible religious experiences. The first occurred around the year 400 AD when a monk named Saint Maron began spreading Christianity across Lebanon. His followers continued this work until virtually the entire country had become Christian. The second impact was a much faster change. This was the Muslim Conquest in 636 AD. The invaders quickly seized the low

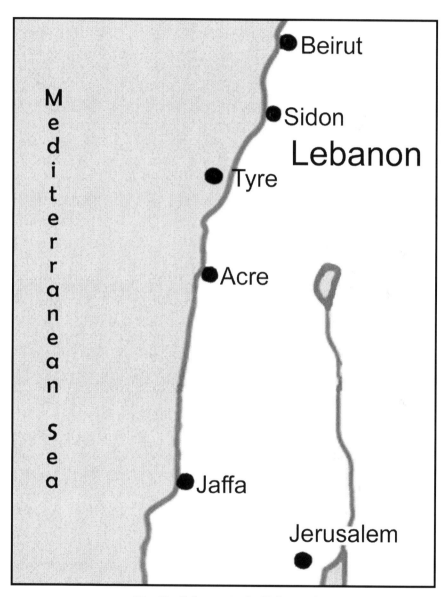

Fig. 23   Lebanon in the Holy Land

lands, and the Christians retreated to the mountain ranges that made up much of the Lebanese countryside.

Crusaders swept across the land in 1099, but then just as quickly most of them went home after Jerusalem was captured. This left the Christians in Lebanon unsure of their fate. That dilemma was resolved when the Knights Templar were formed and began to build protective castles on Lebanese land. Clearly they were here to stay.

Most people do not realize that the Templar brotherhood included seven sergeants for each knight who went off to battle. These sergeants served as infantry, groomed the horses, maintained the armor, and handled all administrative duties. When knights began arriving and sought the Templar cross, large numbers of Lebanese Christians were recruited as sergeants to round out the Templar organization.

It has also rarely been recognized that most of the knights and nobles of Europe at this time were illiterate. They had the ability to sign their name to a document, but that was about the extent of their skill. Almost all of them, including kings, had a clerical person from the church write the document for them, then set it in front of them for signature and seal.

The Lebanese businessmen, however, had been writing since the days they brought their Phoenician alphabet to Greece. The Lebanese did not write great epics, but only dusty journals. Yet they wrote. And as it turned out, the ability of Lebanese entrepreneurs to charm a customer, negotiate an agreement, and write a durable charter conveying property to its new owner was among the best in the East or in the West.

The role of these "clerical" men—who later wore green robes within this Order—has traditionally been overlooked in describing the activities of the Templars.

When Hugh and his four accompanying knights came to Europe to solidly establish the foundation of their organization, they would have brought roughly thirty-five sergeants as well, if they kept to the normal ratio among the Templars. Some of these brothers would have been retainers to ensure the knights were properly outfitted and fed, but the rest would have been the administrators and scribes needed for a successful diplomatic mission of this nature.

To this latter group fell the task of accompanying the Grand Master and handling details of the contracts and diplomacy that were required. Vague promises of support had to be gently nudged into formal commitments and signed documents. What the Grand Master could not do without seeming to step below his noble class, his enterprising sergeants from the Holy Land could do effortlessly and with the confidence born of experience.

Now that we have so clearly seen the support of the former Count of Champagne, it should come as no surprise that one of the first visits paid by the Grand Master and his quiet associates was to Champagne's new Count, Theobald de Blois. That man gave a generous donation of lands at Barbonne, twenty-five miles northwest of Troyes.

Numerous other visits followed in the north of France, each time accompanied by a donation of land, gold, or revenue rights in some form. To assure the proper transfer of title and flow of income from the lands, the Templars developed a practice of leaving behind a few brothers to manage the estates and rights. Over time this was formed into a network of preceptories[27] and estates that became one of their hallmarks. A few of these men-left-behind were knights, but most were drawn from among the sergeants—some who were clerical and some who were tradesmen—due to the nature of the work and the need to have most of the knights serve in the Holy Land.

To point out one other remarkable facet of these events which traditional accounts never mention—why on earth would lords and ladies across Europe throw open their door to the leader of a few knights who had only ruled a small town in his own name? More than that, why would they endow him with rich and valuable estates and heavy weights of gold?

Clearly they were not doing it for him. They were doing it for the man who had stood second in power to the king of France. Not only that, Hugh de Champagne was related to many of these lords and ladies through the intermarriage of families. With de Payens having such a sponsor, they had to open their door to him. And once the first few had given rich gifts, the rest became pressured by social grace to give at least the same. After making the easy appeals first, de Payens moved up to the more challenging targets.

In Northern France he paid a critical visit to King Henry I of England, who was also the Duke of Normandy. Henry was apparently in residence at his Norman estates at the time. The *Anglo-Saxon Chronicle*, written by English scribes during those days, reported the encounter this way.

> This same year (1128 AD), Hugh of the Temple came from Jerusalem to the king in Normandy, and the king received him with much honour, and gave him much treasure in gold and silver, and afterwards he sent him into England, and there he was well received by all good men, and all gave him treasure, and in Scotland also, and they sent in all a great sum in gold and silver by him to Jerusalem, and there went with him and after him so great a number as never before since the days of Pope Urban.[28]

Going to England as the king urged, de Payens and his men were gifted with rich manor-lands by different lords and ladies, including the Old Temple grounds in London. Those Old Temple lands were just south of High Holborn along Chancery Lane, and gradually became the primary preceptory or headquarters for the Templars in England.

The knight they left behind served as the Prior—later called Master—of the Temple in England. With him were a number of administrative brothers who began to draw revenue from the English estates and forward that gold to the Holy Land. The building of a round Templar Church on this large estate commenced shortly thereafter.

Meanwhile, the Grand Master and his remaining brothers continued northward into Scotland. There they received additional gifts of land that included the fair property of Balantrodoch south of Edinburgh. At that place they established their preceptory in Scotland, and commissioned a more modest church. Their local headquarters was similarly on a more modest scale, perhaps beginning to reflect how much their administrative resources were being stretched by that point.

With all these things secured, de Payens hurried back to France to attend the critical Council of Troyes

Council of Troyes
and Templar Secrecy

At this grand council in Troyes, the city where two young men named Hugh began their close relationship many years earlier, de Payens discovered that Bernard of Clairvaux had prepared the stage well.

The distinguished assembly of church leaders listened attentively as de Payens described the existing organization of the Knights Templar, as well as its current religious vows and practices. The strictness of his men's voluntary obligations was apparently quite pleasing to the assembled religious leaders. As a result, the council asked Bernard to draw up a formal religious "Rule" to guide the Templars.[29] This was a traditional step in officially forming a monastic order, and generally was based on an existing Rule, with modifications added to meet the specific needs of the order. Since Bernard was a "friend in court" for the Templars, the Rule for them strongly resembled the practices they were already performing.

One of their specific needs was to acknowledge the clerical administrators who had shown their value to the Templars during the fundraising expedition. They were already being distinguished from the other brothers by being given the title of chaplain. They now began to receive additional rewards alongside the knights, such as this part of the Templar Rule.

> [Section] X. Let a repast of flesh three times a week suffice you, excepting at Christmas, or Easter, or the feast of the Blessed Mary, or of All Saints.... On Sunday we think it clearly fitting and expedient that two messes of flesh should be served up to the knights and the chaplains. But let the rest, to wit, the esquires and retainers, remain contented with one, and be thankful therefor.[30]

When the proceedings of the council were completed, and the appropriate blessings of the council members and the pope had been given, Hugh de Payens and the other Templars prepared for their return to the Holy Land. The Grand Master set sail at the head of many newly-recruited knights, aboard ships laden with heavy loads of gold and silver. He left behind in France, England and Scotland small contingents of men to oversee the many scattered manors and lands he had accumulated. Those brothers were charged with turning the properties into productive estates, and sending more boatloads of gold and silver to Jerusalem for support of the growing phenomenon known as the Knights Templar.

To mark their official letters and communications, the Templars developed a seal which has become a widely-recognized symbol of their order. The portrayal of two knights on a horse is often confused with being a portrayal of their poverty. That is a common misconception. The individual knights took vows of poverty, but the Order itself was rich. Even in their early days, Saint Bernard recorded in his Rule that each knight should content himself with three horses, unless the Grand Master felt that the knight should have more.[31]

So if that does not explain their symbol, what would explain it? As one suggestion, take a look at the seal for the Count of Champagne shown here. It portrays a knight on horseback. Then look at the Templar symbol of two men on horseback. Do you notice any similarity?

*Fig. 24 Seal of the Count of Champagne (above)
seal of the Knights Templar (below)*

If the Templar seal was modeled on the one belonging to the Count of Champagne—then might the two men on the horse be Hugh de Champagne and Hugh de Payens, the two lifelong friends who played leading roles in founding the Knights Templar?

Ten years after the Council of Troyes, pope Innocent II recognized the escalating prominence of the Knights Templar by yielding additional concessions to them. These were spelled out clearly in his official letter *Omne datum optimum.* Among other things, this remarkable document made the Templars exempt from the laws and rulers of every country, owing their allegiance only to the pope. Their properties in different lands became part of an international domain that could not be touched.

In the long, slow rise of the Vatican's power from its small beginnings, this was an amazing declaration of how far it had come. The pope now possessed such a high level of authority that he could direct the kings of Europe on what they could and could not do in this matter. And it involved something near and dear to the heart of those kings—their revenue. He declared that those things which came into the possession of the Templars could not be touched by any ruler, nor be taxed by them.

There was another provision in the papal order that was essential to the Templars and the powerful people they would become, but has been largely overlooked by outsiders. The pope's declaration granted a special privilege for the clerical brothers within the Templar Order in recognition of the critical role they served. In addition to their previous rights as chaplains—reading the bible at prayer meetings, writing correspondence and counseling the other brothers—they were now allowed to be ordained and serve as priests.[32] With this, they put on their green robes marked with a red cross, and became a distinct group among the Templars.

This was a pivotal milestone for the Templars and the secrecy in which they began to wrap themselves. The granting of priestly rights to some of the Templar brothers finally allowed them to eliminate outsiders from any role in their affairs. Prior to this time, the Templars had been required to use priests from local parishes.

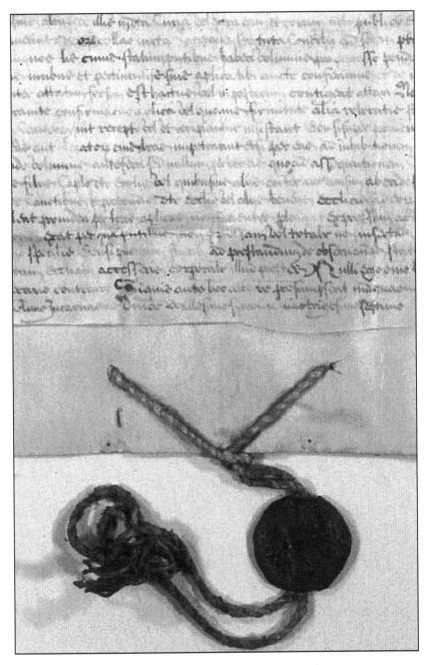

*Fig. 25   This official letter or bull issued by the pope
is like the one issued for the Templars*

Those outsiders were the ones who listened to the confessions of the Templar brothers, hearing their innermost secrets. Those parish priests also wrote some of the letters for the brothers, and had access to all the records and communications in each Templar headquarters.

All of that changed with the pope's order. Men who were Templar clerks could now be ordained, hear those confessions, provide the religious element in all private meetings, and have sole access to the Templar records.[33] The outside priests were escorted to the door, the door was closed behind them, and the key was turned. That was the last any outsider ever knew about the ever-more secretive internal affairs of the Knights Templar

With these powers granted to them, the Templars now had everything they needed to shape the incredibly rich and influential future which lay ahead of them.

They had a foundation built by the man who was second in power and authority to the king of France. That man, Hugh de Champagne, had used his lands and wealth well, including his endowment of Bernard with an abbey at Clairvaux. Bernard in turn built up that abbey and crafted a reputation strong enough to have great influence with the pope. De Champagne had the quasi-royal social standing that opened doors of the rich and famous and motivated them to give gifts of estates and gold to the Templars, starting a flow that would virtually never end.

And the Templars had their other great strength, the charismatic leader and highly-qualified knight Hugh de Payens. He took all that was given to him and made the Templars into an already-rich and powerful society in his own lifetime. He readily attracted not only the necessary gifts, but also the even more necessary knights to expand and populate this new Order. He led those brave men to victories on fields of battle. And he set a high bar for the Grand Masters who followed him.

In all of these things one cannot forget divine providence. How could two such capable men have been born within seven miles of each other—and within four years of each other? This made it possible for them to grow up as trusted friends. That bond of brotherhood proved to be strong enough to last a lifetime—and became an example for the knights in the larger brotherhood they created. It was a trust so strong that the man who was second only to kings could swear to serve his former vassal, and accept him as Grand Master.

These knights also served a very powerful man—the pope. The influence of the Bishop of Rome had grown shockingly over the years. From modest beginnings, the early popes received earthly wealth when they were given the Papal States in Italy. Then they gained political power by anointing Charlemagne as emperor, thereby taking on the role of kingmaker when other kings sought similar treatment. The popes became international leaders when they called for the Crusades and saw princes surge forward to do their bidding. And they became a true military power when the Knights Templar appeared, and agreed to directly serve the pope.

These were the unique origins of the knights of Solomon's Temple. It all began with two remarkable men, the hand of God, and popes who had the power to grant their wishes. With those things in place, the Knights Templar began their long and adventurous ride to glory and tragedy.

It was a journey with banners waving in the wind above them, and then with flames leaping high around them. Their lives and experiences have continued to stir hearts and imaginations even down to the present day.

The rest of the intriguing story of the Templars—their resplendent glory, the tragic fall in 1307, and their fascinating survival after that persecution—is told in the book *Sworn in Secret.*

Appendix

Fig. 26   Tomar Castle of the Knights Templar in Portugal,
including the round Convento de Christo church

Templars
and the Reconquista

$\mathcal{T}$he battles fought by the Templars were not confined to the Holy Land. Among the many gifts they received were estates in the Iberian peninsula, which inevitably dragged them into the Reconquista that was still being actively fought in that land.

The first castle received by the Templars in this troubled region was at Soure near Coimbra, which was halfway between Porto and Lisbon and on the frontier of Christian lands.[34] This gift came from Countess Teresa of Portugal in 1128 when Hugh de Payens was riding across Europe soliciting the first donation of estates from the rulers and lords of many countries. So even from their earliest days the Templars had a stake in what was happening there.

Of course, Hugh and his Templars were too busy trying to establish themselves in the Holy Land to do much in these Iberian lands, but that changed as they became more secure in the East. And the inducements offered by Christian rulers in Spain and Portugal became steadily more enticing. In 1130 Count Ramon Berenguer III of Barcelona gave them a castle at Grañena, followed four years later by a most incredible gift from King Alfonso I of Aragon and Navarre.

He left his entire kingdom—which spread all along the Pyrenees mountains—to the Templars, Hospitallers, and Church of the Holy Sepulchre in Jerusalem, to be divided up among them. This was not acceptable to the people of Aragon nor to the citizens of Navarre. After long negotiations, the Hospitallers and Church of the Holy Sepulchre dropped out. In 1143 the Templars ceded their possible rights to the kingdom in exchange for many castles and revenues in Aragon, as well as a share of any Muslim territories conquered by that kingdom. In this way the Templars became directly, and profitably, involved in the Reconquista.

Meanwhile, far to the west in the lands of the Count of Portugal, the Templars received a major estate in the capital city of Braga. This increased when Count Alfonso won several military battles which extend his territory, and declared himself King of Portugal. From that time forward Portugal was separate from Spain, and was its own nation. When Alfonso captured Lisbon in 1147, he donated part of this conquest to the Templars.

But an even more spectacular event happened in 1159 when Alfonso gave a large expanse of land to the Templars at a place that would become known as Tomar. There the knights industriously set about building a magnificent castle and church, as well as a town to service their new creation. Tomar became the headquarters of the Templars in Portugal. This massive castle and its round church—the Convento de Christo—still stand there today.

As the kingdoms of Portugal, León & Castile, and Aragon—which now included Catalonia—pressed southward, the Templars were always on the leading edge of the fighting. And they continued to be rewarded with more lands and castles as victories were won.

By 1307, all of the Iberian peninsula had been recovered by the Reconquista except for the kingdom of Granada at its southern tip. Then the Templars were attacked by the king of France and by their own pope, who put them on trial and burned many of them at the stake. King Dinis of Portugal protected the knights who were in his kingdom at that time, but this attack on the Templars knocked them out of the Reconquista.

In 1492 King Ferdinand and Queen Isabella completed the conquest of Granada and the Reconquista came to an end. While celebrating their victory in January of that year, the king and queen received an explorer named Christopher Columbus, and agreed to finance his trip to the New World. But that's another story.

*Fig. 27   King Ferdinand and Queen Isabella
receive Christopher Columbus*

Appendix B

Templar Castles, Churches & Fortresses

The Knights Templar had 870 estates which were scattered all across Europe and the Holy Land. A surprising number of those castles, churches and fortresses still exist today, and almost all of them are in open view. Many of them are also open to the public so you can go inside and walk where the Templars walked. The castle that constituted their headquarters in Ireland has been converted into a well-appointed hotel, so you can even sleep where the Templars slept, if you so choose.

Scotland

The walls of the old stone church at the Templar headquarters in Scotland still stand in the town of Temple (Balantrodoch) nine miles south of Edinburgh. It is four miles east of Rosslyn Chapel and the castle of the St. Clair family.

Ireland

Clontarf Castle in Dublin served as the Templar headquarters for Ireland, and it is now the Clontarf Castle Hotel. The old Templar church is found by walking counter-clockwise around the block.

England

Temple Church is still actively in use in London, on the Inner Temple grounds which housed their headquarters for England. See the separate chapter on "Templar Preceptory in London."

The Cressing Temple barns are monumental wooden structures still standing on a Medieval farm 140 miles northeast of London. They reflect the wealth that was earned on the Templar estates.

Garway Church is in Herefordshire, 40 miles north of Bristol, with its solid Templar church tower, built around 1200 AD.

In the part of Cornwall known as Bodmin Moor stands the stone Templar church built on their property in 1120 AD, where the small town adjacent to it is today called Temple.

France

In Paris, the site of the Templar fortress is now covered by the city hall for the 3rd arrondissement, and by the adjoining gardens on Rue du Temple, which are reached via the nearby Temple Metro station.

Sainte Eulalie de Cernon has a magnificently preserved Templar commandery in a Medieval setting in the south of France 50 miles from the Mediterranean Sea.

La Couvertoirade is another well-preserved Templar town and fortress located only ten miles southeast of Sainte Eulalie.

A beautiful Templar chapel is located in the town of Laon about 80 miles northeast of Paris; it was built in 1180 AD.

A similar Templar chapel was built in the city of Metz, about 120 miles east of Laon, to serve the knights' preceptory there.

*Fig. 28   The Templar commandery at Sainte Eulalie de Cernon
in France includes this round church*

Fig. 29 Templar mansion in Italy, known as Castello della Magione.
Their church is on the right, in front of the courtyard.

Italy

Castello della Magione is a Templar mansion that is still in use at Poggibonsi, 26 miles south of Florence. It includes a church and an inner, protected courtyard.

Complesso Templare di San Bevignate is a church and adjoining Templar buildings in Perugia, 90 miles north of Rome.

Valvisciolo Abbey is a church and attached buildings, 40 miles southeast of Rome. After the Templars were attacked in 1307 it became a Cistercian monastery and is still used by them today. It is possible to visit the church and cloister.

Spain

The incredible Castillo do los Templarios at Ponferrada is a bit off the beaten path in northwestern Spain, 60 miles west of the Medieval royal city of León, but it's worth the trip.

The Iglesia Vera Cruz (Church of the True Cross) is in Segovia, 50 miles north of Madrid, and the Templars built it to hold a piece of the cross on which Jesus died. The small relic is now in the nearby church at Zamarramala. The church tower looks over the old city.

The impressive Templar fortress at Peniscola is 70 miles north of Valencia and is built on a peninsula that sticks out into the blue Mediterranean Sea. The 1961 movie *El Cid* was filmed here, and a recent episode of *Game of Thrones*. It is a popular vacation spot.

Portugal

The crown jewel of Templar castles in Portugal is their headquarters at Tomar, 80 miles north of Lisbon, along with its spectacular Convento de Christo church. *(See Figure 26)*

Clustered nearby are three other picturesque towns with their own Templar fortifications:

*Fig. 30   The Templar fortress at Peniscola in Spain
extends out into the Mediterranean Sea*

- Dornes Tower, 16 miles north of Tomar.

- Idanha-a-Velha Tower, 90 miles to the east of Tomar.

- Almourol Castle, 14 miles south of Tomar is a must-see beauty located on a small island in the middle of the Tagus River.

Israel

In Jerusalem, on Temple Mount, the worldwide headquarters of the Templars is still visible in the three massive central arches they built as the entryway to what is now called Al Aqsa Mosque. The Templars kept their horses in the chamber under the Mount which came to be known as Solomon's Stables, and was reached by stairs descending down into the Mount.

The huge Templar encampment in the old town of Acre was largely destroyed, but the remarkable secret tunnel they built underground to connect their fortifications can still be visited today.

Syria

Chastel Blanc (the White Castle) stands in Safita, 12 miles north of the border with Lebanon. From the roof of this massive tower could once be seen the Hospitaller fortress Krac des Chevaliers and the Templar fortifications at Tartus.

In the seaport of Tartus, the entire northwest quarter of the old city was a Templar citadel. Those thick walls were later adapted into homes and other buildings so they can still be seen today.

Arwad Island, just offshore from Tartus, holds a fortress used by the Templars in their attempts to re-gain the Holy Land.

Templar Preceptory
in London

When Hugh de Payens, first Grand Master of the Knights Templar, toured England and Scotland in 1128 to recruit knights and donations to support the Templars' mission in the Holy Land, his efforts began in London. There he was soon rewarded with a particularly attractive bequest: an expanse of property between the walled city of London and the Abbey at Westminster. It was among the fields which would become known as Holborn, a half-mile north of the River Thames.

On it he established the Templars' headquarters in England, and immediately began to raise a round church—a practice that would become one of the identifying marks of the men he led. As their fortunes improved, the Templars in London purchased an even larger property directly to the south. This gave them all the land from what is now Fleet Street to the River Thames, extending from Temple Avenue in the east to about Essex Street in the west. This area is still called Temple to the present day. A larger, round Temple Church was raised there by these men in 1185, and it continues to be regularly open for services.

Charles G. Addison, who worked on what remained of the Temple properties in 1874, described those events this way.

*Fig. 31 Temple Church was built by the Templars in 1185
and still stands in London*

The Knights Templars had first established the chief house of their Order in England, without Holborn Bars,[35] on the south side of the street, where Southampton House formerly stood, adjoining to which Southampton Buildings were afterwards erected; and it is stated, that about a century and a half ago,[36] part of the ancient chapel annexed to this establishment, of a circular form, and built of Caen stone, was discovered on pulling down some old houses near Southampton Buildings in Chancery Lane. This first house of the Temple, established by Hugh de Payens himself, before his departure from England, A.D. 1130, on his return to Palestine, was adapted to the wants and necessities of the Order in its infant state, when the Knights, instead of lingering in the Preceptories of Europe, proceeded at once to Palestine, and when all the resources of the society were strictly and faithfully forwarded to Jerusalem, to be expended in defense of the faith. But when the Order had greatly increased in numbers, power, and wealth, and had somewhat departed from its original purity and simplicity, we find that the Superior and the Knights resident in London began to look abroad for a more extensive and commodious place of habitation. They purchased a large space of ground, extending from the White Friars westward to Essex House without Temple Bar, and commenced the erection of a convent on a scale of grandeur commensurate with the dignity and importance of the chief house of the great religio-military society of the Temple in Britain. It was called the *New* Temple, to distinguish it from the original establishment at Holborn, which came thenceforth to be known by the name of the *Old* Temple. This New Temple was adapted for the residence of numerous military monks and novices, serving brothers, retainers, and domestics. It contained the residence of the Superior and of the Knights, the cells and apartments of the chaplains and serving brethren, the council chamber where the

Chapters were held,[37] and the refectory or dining-hall, which was connected by a range of handsome cloisters with the magnificent Church, consecrated by the Patriarch. Alongside the river extended a spacious pleasure-ground for the recreation of the brethren, who were not permitted to go into the town without the leave of the Master. It was used also for military exercises and the training of horses.[38]

The fall of the Templars in 1307 caused those magnificent halls, cloisters and dormitories to be handed over to others, then be leased to members of the legal profession, who occupy it still. Two Inns of Court—which call legal professionals to the Bar and enable them to practice as barristers—occupy what is almost the entirety of the former New Temple property. These Inns are known as Inner Temple and Middle Temple.[39] The remainder of the property extending westward is called Outer Temple, and has been mainly given over to commercial buildings. On Fleet Street one enters a gated archway and walks south toward Temple Church, passing beside the buildings of the Inner Temple, which have been largely rebuilt since the days of the Templars. Looming on the left is Temple Church, the knights' main legacy. It still stands as they built it, though repairs have been made during the seven centuries since men clothed in white mantles and red crosses last walked there.

One other ancient fragment remains, however, and it is found straight ahead, just south of the Church. A long building stands where the Templars' magnificent main hall once arrayed itself, and in fact the west end of that ancient building was retained and is part of the current structure. The several walls of weathered stone seen there constituted the "buttery" part of the Templar dining hall. This venerable collection of rooms remains an actively-used part of Inner Temple Hall. Farther west from the hall are the many buildings of the Middle Temple. Upon reaching Middle Temple Lane, if one turns south and follows the road downhill toward the Thames, an archway pierces through the connected buildings at or near the location of the original gate from the Templar properties. The walled-off privacy and grandeur of the

Inner Temple and Middle Temple buildings still evoke the presence of the confident and lordly Knights Templar who once lived and feasted in these halls.

Fig. 32   The remaining part of the original Templar dining hall

Templar Gold

*T*emplar gold brought many good things to the knights of Solomon's Temple, but it also brought one devastating result, as shown in this excerpt from the book *Sworn in Secret*.

> Powerful men were at work in Europe, most notably Philip IV of France who was engaged in manipulating the popes and the battlefields of the continent. King Philip was surnamed "the Fair" because of his handsome appearance—certainly not for any deference to justice on his part. Philip inherited two things upon his father's untimely death during a failed war in Spain: a crushing war debt, and a lavish lifestyle. To make matters worse, Philip began a new war of his own with England. As his debt mushroomed, the heavy-handed monarch sought a measure of relief by aggressively taxing his people and the Christian clergy in France.
>
> Objecting to this taxation of the clergy, Pope Boniface VIII ordered that no such levy could be made without the consent of the pope. He followed this with

an official letter asserting that the pope had higher authority than any king. Philip responded by having the Pope captured and so severely beaten that he died a month later in October of 1303.

The successor to Boniface was Benedict XI, who lived only eight months in office before dying under conditions often described as suspicious.

Philip then arranged to have a French archbishop chosen as pope. This was Clement V. The new pontiff apparently decided dying young was not appealing, and proceeded to give King Philip almost everything he wanted. This would work to the severe detriment of the Templars. As a sign of his loyalty, Clement moved the seat of the Church from Rome to France, eventually settling at Avignon near Marseille.

Pope Clement was the direct superior to Templar Grand Master Jacques de Molay. For that reason it put de Molay in an extremely difficult position when the pontiff proposed merging the Templars and Hospitallers into a single order. To be fair, this idea was not original with Clement. Moreover, with no ongoing victories in the Holy Land, there was little justification to maintain two large military orders. Even so, it was another cross for the Grand Master to bear.

Not to be outdone by the pope, the French king also began to cast a desirous eye upon the Knights Templar. Philip's finances, already depleted by the war with England, now suffered further losses from a war with Flanders. The Templars were involved in helping to finance these ventures because they were authorized by Philip to collect various taxes owed to him. Those amounts were then stored in the Templar treasury at Paris until the funds were disbursed as he directed.[40]

In a dark foreshadowing of events to come, Philip fed his need for funds by seizing the property and persons of Italian bankers from Lombardy in 1291. He

Fig. 33 The Paris fortress of the Knights Templar

applied the same harsh measures to Jews in France in 1306, pressing their assets into his treasury.

That same year Philip admitted to having reduced the weight of silver coins in his realm, which ruined their value, and overnight the French currency was worth only a third of what it was before. Violent riots broke out in Paris, forcing the king to take refuge in the fortress of the Templar preceptory.[41] The Templars of Paris took Philip in and protected him without complaint. Unfortunately, the king's manipulation of the coinage of the realm had created an immediate need for more gold and silver—and his majesty had several days to sit in the richly appointed Templar buildings while thinking about where he might obtain it.

Philip's coveting of Templar gold would soon bring a tragic day of reckoning.

Illuminated with 100 photographs, maps and works of art, *Sworn in Secret* is an intriguing voyage through the dark, hidden chambers of the Knights Templar and their impact on the world in which we live today.

Illustrations, Acknowledgements

Figure

Figure

11 Peter the Hermit Preaching the People's Crusade (painting by James Archer, 1822-1904)

12 The Leaders of the Prince's Crusade (from *History of France*, by François Guizot, 1869, illustrated by Alphonse de Neuville)

13 Map of The Princes' Crusade from Europe to Jerusalem (Holst)

14 Florine of Burgundy, on the First Crusade (engraving by Gustave Doré, 1832-1883)

15 Baldwin entering Edessa (painting by Joseph-Nicolas Robert-Fleury, 1840)

16 The cathedral in Troyes, where a religious council was held as an essential step in forming the Knights Templar — original photo was by DXR Daniel Vorndran/CC-BY-SA-3.0.

17 The Benedictine abbey at Monte Cassino (courtesy of Nato Communications and Information Systems School)

18 Saint Bernard of Clairvaux (painting by Georg Andreas Wasshuber , 1650-1732)

19 The Templars built these arches on the front of Al Aqsa mosque when they used it as their headquarters — original photo was by Mark A. Wilson.

20 The Holy Grail (from *Our Young Folks*, an illustrated magazine, edited by J.T. Trowbridge, Lucy Larcom and Gail Hamilton, Boston: Ticknor and Fields, 1866)

21 Ark of the Covenant (painting by James Jacques Joseph Tissot, 1836-1902)

22 Abbey of Saint Bernard at Clairvaux (courtesy of the City Library of Troyes)

23 Map of Lebanon in the Holy Land (Holst)

24 Seal of the Count of Champagne *(above)*—from *Voyage archéologique et pittoresque dans le département de l'Aube et dans l'ancien diocèse de Troyes* by Anne Francois Arnaud, 1837. Seal of the Knights Templar *(below)*—from *Sketch of the History of the Knights Templars* by James Burnes, 1840.

25 An official letter or bull like this one was issued about the Templars (from a papal bull by Pope Urban VIII, 1637)

Figure

26 Tomar Castle of the Knights Templar in Portugal, including the round Convento de Christo church—original photo was by Alvesgaspar/CC-BY-SA-4.0.

27 King Ferdinand and Queen Isabella receive Christopher Columbus (painting by Emanuel Leutze, 1843)

28 The Templar commandery at Sainte Eulalie de Cernon in France includes this round church—original photo was by Castanet/CC-BY-SA-2.5.

29 Templar mansion in Italy, known as Castello della Magione. Their church is on the right, in front of the courtyard—original photo was by Thomas Hooker.

30 The Templar fortress at Peniscola in Spain extends out into the Mediterranean Sea—original photo was by Grodin.tierce/CC-BY-SA-3.0.

31 Temple Church was built by the Templars in 1185 and still stands in London (Holst)

32 The remaining part of the original Templar dining hall (Holst)

33 The Paris fortress of the Knights Templar (from *Sketch of the History of the Knights Templars* by James Burnes, 1840)

Annotations

1 Barber, Malcolm *The New Knighthood.* (Cambridge: Cambridge University Press, 1994), p. 179, in which he cites A. Stewart *Anonymous Pilgrims.* (London: Palestine Pilgrims' Text Society 6, 1894), Vol. 2, pp. 29-30.

2 The first Grand Master of the Knights Templar is most commonly known in English as Hugh de Payens, yet the French prefer Hugues de Payns, with other variations also occurring. Since he came from the town of Payns in the Champagne region of France, there is some logic behind the French usage. His service in the Holy Land is discussed in later notes.

3 Addison, Charles G. *The History of the Knights Templars.* (London: Longman, Brown, Green & Longmans, 1842).

4 Barber, Malcolm *The New Knighthood.* (Cambridge: Cambridge University Press, 1994).

5 Godfrey ruled the kingdom of Jerusalem, but preferred the modest title "Advocate of the Holy Sepulchre." The men who succeeded him were not as modest and used the title of king.

[6] McKitterick, Rosamond editor. *The New Cambridge Medieval History.* (Cambridge: University of Cambridge Press, 1995), Vol. II, pp. 258-271.

[7] Gibbon, Edward. *The History of the Decline and Fall of the Roman Empire.* (Philadelphia: Birch & Small, 1804).

[8] O'Callaghan, Joseph F. *A History of Medieval Spain.* (Ithaca, NY: Cornell University Press, 1975), p.40.

[9] The rape of Julian's daughter, whose name was given as Florinda La Cava, was addressed in many Medieval writings. It was even included in *Don Quixote* by Miguel de Cervantes.

[10] Gibralter also received its name at this time. It came from the Arabic words *Jabal Tariq*, which meant "mountain of Tariq," having been named after the invading Muslim leader. Over time this became *Jabaltar* then *Gibraltar*. Hills, George. *Rock of Contention: A history of Gibraltar.* (London: Robert Hale & Company, 1974), p. 13.

[11] Hanson, Victor Davis. *Culture and Carnage: Landmark Battles in the Rise of Western Power.* (New York: Doubleday, 2001), pp. 135-169

[12] The letter *chi* is translated as "ch" and the letter *rho* as "r"—these are the first letters in the name of Christ.

[13] The Battle of Manzikert in 1071.

[14] The first great writing in Castilian Spanish was *El Cantar de mio Cid*, an epic poem about this knight, consisting of 3730 verses written between 1140 and 1207 AD.

[15] Edgington, Susan, and Sarah Lambert, editors. *Gendering the Crusades.* (New York: Columbia University Press, 2002), pp. 53–54. A romanicized account of Florine's life was published in 1855 by William Bernard MacCabe as *Princess of Burgundy*.

[16] Addison, Charles G. *The History of the Knights Templars.* (London: Longman, Brown, Green & Longmans, 1842), p. 11.

[17] In formal usage he would be addressed as Hugh, Count of Champagne, but that is modified here to the more familiar Hugh de Champagne.

[18] Barber, *The New Knighthood*, note 21 on p.336. Also lamop.univ-paris1.fr/baudin/anglais/comtes/hugues/ hugues.htm retrieved 23 Aug 2008. Albéric gives the dates of Hugh de Champagne's visits to the Holy Land as 1113, 1121 and 1125, but the impacts on his life and the Knights Templar were the same.

[19] Sainthood is only granted after a person's death, but St. Bernard was so well known by that name that it is occasionally used to refer to him during his life as well.

[20] Barber, Malcolm. *The New Knighthood: A History of the Order of the Temple.* (Cambridge: Cambridge University Press, 1994), pp. 9-10, who cited Albert of Aix, "Historia Hierosolymitana" in *RHCr. Occid*, Vol. IV, 12.33, pp. 712-713.

[21] William of Tyre gave the founding year for the Templars as 1118, but he wrote many years after the event, and provided no supporting evidence. Malcolm Barber cited several documents written within nine years of the founding of the Templars, which point to 1119—or at the latest January 1120—as the proper founding date. Barber, Malcolm. *The New Knighthood*, pp. 8-9.

[22] Barber, Malcolm. *The New Knighthood*, p. 9. In which he refers to Hiestand.

[23] Also known as Geoffrey de St. Aldemar.

[24] Andre de Montbard was the uncle of St. Bernard.

[25] Bernard of Clairvaux. *Epistolae, in Sancti Bernardi Opera*, editors J. Leclercq and H. Rochais, Vol. VII, (Rome: 1974), ep. 31, pp. 85-86; in Barber, *The New Knighthood*, p. 11.

[26] Addison, *The History of the Knights Templars*, p. 13.

[27] In each region one estate was designated to house the leading Templar officials in that area, provide financial services, and watch over the smaller estates. Known as a preceptory, it could oversee anything from a small area to an entire country.

[28] Addison, *The History of the Knights Templars*, p. 26.

[29] Addison *The History of the Knights Templars*, pp. 13-14.

[30] *The Rule of the Poor Fellow-soldiers of Jesus Christ and of the Temple of Solomon*, Section X, as shown in Addison *The History of the Knights Templars*, p. 17.

[31] Section XXX of the Templar Rule.

[32] Per papal bull *Omne datum optimum* (1139); Barber, *The New Knighthood*, p.195-198.

[33] Barber, *The New Knighthood*, pp. 197-198, shows the Templars went to great lengths to confess only to their own chaplains, and that this was one of the charges against them at their trial—that they did it to hide heresy. In their own defense, the Templars could only cite a few cases in which they confessed to outside priests, and

some of those priests were tightly aligned with the Templars in other ways.

[34] Selwood, Dominic. *Knights of the Cloister: Templars and Hospitallers in Central-southern Occitania 1100-1300.* (Woodbridge, UK: Boydell Press, 1999), p. 35.

[35] In those days the walled city of London referred to its gates as "bars." The usage here refers to being just outside Holborn gate from the walled city of that time, on the street now called High Holborn.

[36] About 1724, counting from the date of his writing.

[37] Religious orders often referred to the Abbot and monks in a location as a Chapter, and frequently had a special place to hold their Chapter meetings. For example, Westminster Abbey and York Minster both have Chapter Houses attached to their cathedrals.

[38] Addison, Charles G. and Robert Macoy. *The Knights Templar History.* (New York: Masonic Publishing, 1874/1912), pp. 475-476.

[39] The "Inner" Temple buildings were closer to Old London. The "Middle" Temple buildings were slightly farther west.

[40] Barber, *The New Knighthood*, pp. 296-297.

[41] Barber, Malcolm. *The Trial of the Templars.* (Cambridge: Cambridge University Press, 2006), p. 52.

Bibliography

Addison, Charles G. *The History of the Knights Templars* London: Longman, Brown, Green & Longmans, 1842.

_____ and Robert Macoy *The Knights Templar History.* New York: Masonic Publishing, 1874/1912.

Appian. *Wars of the Romans in Iberia.* (Greek, translated into English by J.S. Richardson.) Warminster, UK: Aris & Phillips, 2000.

Asbridge, Thomas *The First Crusade: A New History.* Oxford: Oxford University Press, 2004.

Baigent, Michael, Richard Leigh and Henry Lincoln *Holy Blood, Holy Grail.* New York: Delacorte Press, 1982.

Baigent, Michael and Richard Leigh. *The Temple and the Lodge.* New York: Arcade, 1989.

Baldwin, Marshall W. *A History of the Crusades: The First Hundred Years.* Madison, WI: University of Wisconsin Press, 1969.

Barber, Malcolm. *The Trial of the Templars.* Cambridge: Cambridge University Press, First edition 1978, Second edition 2006.

_____ *The New Knighthood: A History of the Order of the Temple.* Cambridge: Cambridge University Press, 1994.

Bartlett, Robert *The Making of Europe: Conquest, Colonization and Cultural Change 950–1350.* Princeton: Princeton Univ. Press, 1994.

Baynes, Thomas Spencer, editor. *Encyclopaedia Britannica.* New York: Henry G. Allen, 1888.

Bernard of Clairvaux. *Epistolae,* in *Sancti Bernardi Opera.* (ed. J. Leclercq and H. Rochais) Rome: Editiones Cistercienses, 1974.

Boardman, John et al, eds. *The Oxford History of the Roman World.* Oxford: Oxford University Press, 1986.

Burgoyne, Michael Hamilton. "1187 – 1260" in *Where Heaven and Earth Meet: Jerusalem's Sacred Esplanade.* (ed. Oleg Grabar and Benjamin Z. Kedar) Austin: University of Texas Press, 2009.

Burnes, James. *Sketch of the History of the Knights Templars.* Edinburgh: William Blackwood & Sons, 1840.

Cancik, Hubert and Helmuth Schneider, eds. *Brill's New Pauly Encyclopedia of the Ancient World.* Leiden, The Netherlands: Brill, 2002.

Frankopan, Peter *The First Crusade: The Call from the East.* Cambridge, MA: Harvard University Press, 2012.

Gibbon, Edward. *The History of the Decline and Fall of the Roman Empire.* Philadelphia: Birch & Small, 1804.

Gil, Moshe *A History of Palestine, 634–1099.* Cambridge: Cambridge University Press, 1997.

Haag, Michael. *The Templars: The History & the Myth.* New York: Harper, 2009.

Harris, Jonathan *Byzantium and the Crusades.* London: Bloomsbury Publishing, 2014.

Hillenbrand, Carole *The Crusades: Islamic Perspectives.* New York: Routledge, 2000.

Holst, Sanford. *Phoenician Secrets: Exploring the Ancient Mediterranean.* Los Angeles: Santorini Publishing, 2011.

_____ *Sworn in Secret: Freemasonry and the Knights Templar.* Los Angeles: Santorini Publishing, 2012.

Holt, Peter M. *The Age of the Crusades: The Near East from the Eleventh Century to 1517.* Reading, MA: Addison Wesley Longman, 1989.

Housley, Norman *Contesting the Crusades.* Malden, MA: Blackwell Publishing, 2006.

Konstam, Angus *Historical Atlas of the Crusades.* London: Mercury Books, 2004.

Lagassé, Paul et al, eds. *The Columbia Encyclopedia, Sixth Edition.* New York: Columbia University Press, 2001-04.

Lomas, Robert *Turning the Templar Key.* Beverly, MA: Fair Winds Press, 2007.

Lock, Peter *Routledge Companion to the Crusades.* New York: Routledge, 2006.

Madden, Thomas *New Concise History of the Crusades.* Lanham, MD: Rowman & Littlefield, 2005.

Manuel des Chevaliers de l'Ordre du Temple. Paris: Chevaliers de l'Ordre du Temple, 1825.

Mayer, Hans Eberhard *The Crusades.* Translated from German by John Gillingham. Oxford: Oxford University Press, 1988.

McKitterick, Rosamond, editor. *The New Cambridge Medieval History.* Cambridge: University of Cambridge Press, 1995.

Meyers, Eric, ed. *Oxford Encyclopedia of Archaeology in the Near East.* New York: Oxford University Press, 1997.

Neveux, François *The Normans.* Translated from French by Howard Curtis. Philadelphia, PA: Running Press, 2008.

Nicolle, David *The First Crusade, 1096–99: Conquest of the Holy Land.* Botley, OX: Osprey Publishing, 2003.

O'Callaghan, Joseph F. *A History of Medieval Spain.* Ithaca, NY: Cornell University Press, 1975.

Riley-Smith, Jonathan *The First Crusade and the Idea of Crusading.* Philadelphia, PA: University of Pennsylvania, 1991.

_____ *The First Crusaders, 1095–1131.* Cambridge: Cambridge University Press, 1998.

_____ ed. *The Oxford History of the Crusades.* Oxford: Oxford University Press, 2002.

_____ *The Crusades: A History.* New Haven: Yale University Press, 2005.

Ritmeyer, Leen. *The Quest: Revealing the Temple Mount in Jerusalem.* Jerusalem: Carta, 2006.

Robinson, John J. *Born In Blood: The Lost Secrets of Freemasonry.* New York: M. Evans, 1989.

Runciman, Steven *The First Crusade.* Cambridge: Cambridge University Press, 1980.

_____ *A History of the Crusades: Volume 1, The First Crusade and the Foundation of the Kingdom of Jerusalem.* Cambridge: Cambridge University Press, 1987.

Selwood, Dominic. *Knights of the Cloister: Templars and Hospitallers in Central-southern Occitania 1100-1300.* Woodbridge, UK: Boydell Press, 1999.

Treadgold, Warren *A History of the Byzantine State and Society.* Stanford, CA: Stanford University Press, 1997.

Tyerman, Christopher *God's War: A New History of the Crusades.* Cambridge, MA: Belknap Press of Harvard University Press, 2006.

Vryonis, Speros *Decline of Medieval Hellenism in Asia Minor and the Process of Islamization in the Eleventh through Fifteenth Centuries.* Berkeley, CA: University of California Press, 1971.

Index

23231594R00076

Printed in Great Britain
by Amazon